HE HELD
RADICAL
LIGHT

HE HELD
RADICAL
LIGHT

THE ART OF FAITH,
THE FAITH OF ART

CHRISTIAN WIMAN

FARRAR, STRAUS AND GIROUX

NEW YORK

FARRAR, STRAUS AND GIROUX
175 Varick Street, New York 10014

Owing to limitations of space, all acknowledgments for permission
to reprint previously published material can be found on pages 117–118.

Library of Congress Cataloging-in-Publication Data
Names: Wiman, Christian, 1966– author.
Title: He held radical light : the art of faith and the faith of art / Christian
    Wiman.
Other titles: Art of faith and the faith of art
Description: First edition. | New York : Farrar, Straus and Giroux, 2018.
Identifiers: LCCN 2018003844 | ISBN 9780374168469 (hardcover)
Subjects: LCSH: Religion and poetry. | Faith—Poetry. | Poets—Psychology. |
    Death—Psychological aspects. | Spirituality in literature.
Classification: LCC PN1077 .W57 2018 | DDC 814/.54—dc23
LC record available at https://lccn.loc.gov/2018003844

Designed by Gretchen Achilles

Our books may be purchased in bulk for promotional, educational, or business use.
Please contact your local bookseller or the Macmillan Corporate and Premium
Sales Department at 1-800-221-7945, extension 5442, or by e-mail at
MacmillanSpecialMarkets@macmillan.com.

www.fsgbooks.com
www.twitter.com/fsgbooks • www.facebook.com/fsgbooks

1 3 5 7 9 10 8 6 4 2

FOR DONALD HALL

The world does not need to come from a god. For better or worse, the world is here. But it does need to go to one (where is he?), and that is why the poet exists.

—JUAN RAMÓN JIMÉNEZ

HE HELD
RADICAL
LIGHT

stayed up late last night reading the letters of A. R. Ammons, who for years sowed and savored his loneliness in lonely Ithaca. "Keep Ithaka always in your mind," wrote Constantin Cavafy, "Arriving there is what you're destined for." And he did, Ammons, keep that mythical Ithaka in his mind, which is to say in his poems, decade after decade of diaristic ramblings that are as flavorless as old oatmeal this morning, as null and undifferentiated as deep space—then lit up suddenly by a meteoric masterpiece that must have surprised the workaday writer as much as it does the fatigued reader. It is heroic and it is pathetic, like the life of any real writer, I suppose, all the waste space one fills as one can, some with silence, which is often excruciating for the writer, some with noise, which passes that agony along to the reader. And all for what? Those moments of mysterious intrusion, that feeling of collusion with eternity, of life and language riled to the one wild charge:

THE CITY LIMITS

When you consider the radiance, that it does not withhold
itself but pours its abundance without selection into every
nook and cranny not overhung or hidden; when you consider

that birds' bones make no awful noise against the light but
lie low in the light as in a high testimony; when you consider
the radiance, that it will look into the guiltiest

swervings of the weaving heart and bear itself upon them,
not flinching into disguise or darkening; when you consider
the abundance of such resource as illuminates the glow-blue

bodies and gold-skeined wings of flies swarming the dumped
guts of a natural slaughter or the coil of shit and in no
way winces from its storms of generosity; when you consider

that air or vacuum, snow or shale, squid or wolf, rose or lichen,
each is accepted into as much light as it will take, then
the heart moves roomier, the man stands and looks about, the

leaf does not increase itself above the grass, and the dark
work of the deepest cells is of a tune with May bushes
and fear lit by the breadth of such calmly turns to praise.

I met him once, thirty years ago. I was an undergraduate at Washington and Lee University in Virginia, where I
was a member of the last all-male class in the school's two-
hundred-and-fifty-year history. (It was also, I later learned, the
worst class in the school's two-hundred-and-fifty-year history.)
I had arrived alone from far West Texas in my midnight-blue
T-topped screaming-eagle Trans Am, which would hit a hundred and thirty miles an hour for anyone young enough or fool
enough to do it, and which I sadly but promptly sold to pay

for books, boxer shorts (I'd never seen such a thing before), booze, food.

That was always an urgency then: money. I delivered the *Richmond Times-Dispatch* on foot, 6:00 a.m., seven days a week. I worked in the university news office and in the dining hall, served as food manager for a fraternity, strung tennis rackets many evenings in the gym. In one particularly needy season, together with another student who had the means to be the bank (I was the muscle—or, more accurately, the nag), I ran a gambling line for professional football, posting our hieratic odds on the doors of dorms and fraternities and sitting all afternoon dipped in a sort of existential ant bed, feeling the stings of defeat in every other play. It was mortifying at times, but in the way of American intellectuals whose accomplishments are rooted in real dirt, I have made a badge of my embarrassments, and any shame of monetary or mental unfitness—I vividly remember the vertiginous instant that a dean with a patrician mane and mien pointed out to me that my beloved Robert Ludlum books were not "literature"—has faded into an ironic attribute, like "distressed" furniture.

I was a virgin when I heard Ammons read. A virgin of poetry readings, I mean, though the experience was probably more memorable and momentous than the other one. It occurred to me that Ammons might have been equally innocent, and equally confused, as ten minutes into his reading he suddenly stopped and said, "You can't possibly be enjoying this," then left the podium and sat back down in the front row. No one knew what to do. Some people protested from the pews—we were in a place that had pews—that they were in fact enjoying it, though the voices lacked conviction and he didn't budge. Finally the chair of the English Department (another mane, another mien) cajoled the poor poet into continuing. Ammons mumbled on for another fifteen minutes before the cold mortification of the modern poetry reading, and the beer-lacquered bafflement of press-ganged undergraduates, did him in. "Enough," he muttered finally, and thudded his colossal body down beside his wife like the death of faith itself.

WHEN I LEFT COLLEGE and set out to be a poet I thought of nothing but writing a poem that would live forever. That's just how I phrased it: live forever. It seemed to me the only noble ambition, and its fumes were evident in my contempt for the lesser aims I sniffed out in other writers. It was, I suppose, a transparent attempt to replace the soul with the self—for all the talk of the "extinction of personality," I suspect there is no artist who does not cling to the belief that something essential of himself inheres in his art—and it was the first casualty of Christianity for me. People tend to think that Christians feel rescued from death, and perhaps some do (I don't), but first there comes the purge. *Nothing* survives, I suddenly realized. Dante, Virgil, even sweet Shakespeare, whose lines will last as long as there are eyes to read him, will one day find that there are no eyes to read him. As a species, we are a microscopic speck of existence, which, I have full faith, will one day thrive without us.

Still, abstract oblivion is a small shock as shocks go. When over lunch one day my friend and then poet laureate Donald

Hall turned his Camel-blasted eighty-year-old Yeti decrepitude to me and said as casually as he bit into his burger, "I was thirty-eight when I realized not a word I wrote was going to last," I felt a galactic chill, as if my soul had chewed tinfoil. I was thirty-eight. It was the very inverse of a calling, an ex post facto feeling of innocence, death's echo. In a flash I knew it was true, for both of us (this is no doubt part of what he was telling me), and yet the shock was not in that fact but in the nearly fifty years of further writings Don had piled on top of that revelation. "Poetry abandoned me," he writes in his little masterpiece *Essays After Eighty*, the compensatory prose of which is so spare and clear it seems inscribed on solitude itself. If there were any justice in the world, this book would be read by my great-great-great-granddaughter as she gets ready to die. But of course there is no justice in the world.

> They will put my body into the ground.
> Chemistry will have its way for a time,
> and then large beetles will come.
> After that, the small beetles. Then
> the disassembling. After that, the Puccini
> will dwindle the way light goes
> from the sea. Even Pittsburgh will
> vanish, leaving a greed tough as winter.
>
> —JACK GILBERT

What is it we want when we can't stop wanting? I say God, but Jack Gilbert's greed may be equally accurate, at least as long as God is an object of desire rather than its engine, end rather than means. Gilbert's poem amounts to a kind of metaphysics for materialists. *Something* survives us, the poem suggests, some cellular imperative ravening past whatever cohesion kept us, us; some life force that is suspiciously close to a death force: it's winter, after all, and not any ordinary winter but one from which even Puccini and Pittsburgh have vanished, an ur-winter, you might say, even a nuclear one. Of course on the literal level the poem is referring to the way information dies out in one man's brain—Gilbert was actually from Pittsburgh, and I assume he loved Puccini—but the end of the poem reverberates in a way that is both beautiful and terrible. When you are ending, it can seem like everything is, and the last task of some lives is to let the world go on being the world they once loved. But what song—or what but song—can contain *that* tangle of pain and praise?

A.M.

> . . . *And here the dark infinitive to feel,*
> *Which would endure and have the earth be still*
> *And the star-strewn night pour down the mountains*
> *Into the hissing fields and silent towns until the last*
> *Insomniac turned in, must end, and early risers see*
> *The scarlet clouds break up and golden plumes of smoke*
> *From uniform dark homes turn white, and so on down*
> *To the smallest blade of grass and fallen leaf*
> *Touched by the arriving light. Another day has come,*

Another fabulous escape from the damages of night,
So even the gulls, in the ragged circle of their flight,
Above the sea's long lanes that flash and fall, scream
Their approval. How well the sun's rays probe
The rotting carcass of a skate, how well
They show the worms and swarming flies at work,
How well they shine upon the fatal sprawl
Of everything on earth. How well they love us all.

—MARK STRAND

Poetry itself—like life, like love, like any spiritual hunger—thrives on longings that can never be fulfilled, and dies when the poet thinks they have been. And what is true for the poem is true for the poet: "No layoff from this condensery," as Lorine Niedecker says, no respite from the calling that comes in the form of a question, no ultimate arrival at an answer that every arrangement of words is trying to be. Perhaps only bad poets become poets. The good ones, though they may wax vatic and oracular in public, and though they may even have full-fledged masterpieces behind them, know full well that they can never quite claim the name.

Still, there are moments in any writer's life when the movement away from one kind of silence—the kind that keeps your soul suppressed—is decisive. I remember sitting in an empty classroom at Washington and Lee late into the night, working on a poem instead of studying for an exam on international trade. I had spent three years as an economics major: endless afternoons in dead-aired classrooms from which I can't remember a thing in the world except that I *wanted, wanted,*

wanted something so vague it might as well be money. By the time of my last class in the "C-School" I was so hungry for meaning that everything was instantly allegorical—the blind professor who taught international trade, the desk he clung to like a life raft, the random dog that sauntered into that third-floor classroom one afternoon as if he owned the place. He stopped right in front of my desk, turned around twice before taking a disconcertingly deliberate shit, then trotted lightly out like an ironic angel.

Not that the true path was by any means clear. I still had twenty years to writhe on the high hook I knew only as Ambition. It's almost the definition of a calling that there is strong inner resistance to it. The resistance is not practical—how will I make money, can I live with the straitened circumstances, etc.—but existential: Can I navigate this strong current, and can I remain myself while losing myself within it? Reluctant writers, reluctant ministers, reluctant teachers—these are the ones whose lives and works can be examples. Nothing kills credibility like excessive enthusiasm. Nothing poisons truth so quickly as an assurance that one has found it. "The impeded stream is the one that sings." (Wendell Berry)

In 1992 I found myself in Northern California. It was my first year on a Wallace Stegner Fellowship at Stanford and it was Denise Levertov's last year of teaching. She had recently been diagnosed with lymphoma, which I did not realize at the time, and which at any rate would have meant nothing to me aside from the muted and momentary flash of foreboding that you yourself might feel if I told you how that same word—*lymphoma*—would ravage my own life fifteen years later. This is as it should be. Promiscuous sympathy is pointless and damaging for all concerned. That little shiver of pleasure-horror that goes through your spine when you read about someone else's suffering, that quick metaphysical incision like a bone marrow biopsy of the soul: it's for yourself. It *is* your self soundlessly screaming: *I'm going to die!* There's nothing wrong with this—it's one of the functions of literature, to *wake one up*—but if you mistake this reaction for action; if you confuse this shadow sympathy for the kind of real feeling that operates in the world with risk and agency and perhaps even grows cold to survive (bless you, my many marmoreal oncologists); if you mistake love of literature for *love*—well, dear reader, read on, read on.

Denise had recently converted to Catholicism. This I also did not know, though her Christian sensibilities seemed obvious enough. Here is "A Cure of Souls" from 1963:

The pastor
of grief and dreams

guides his flock towards
the next field

with all his care.
He has heard

the bell tolling
but the sheep

are hungry and need
the grass, today and

every day. Beautiful
his patience, his long

shadow, the rippling
sound of the flocks moving

along the valley.

This is not one of Denise's well-known poems, but it does
have its own solid muscle movement and inner necessity: it
stakes a credible claim on the final silence that is the measure
of all made things. And that, finally, defeats all made things?
The poem is aimed at this ultimate question. That valley in

the last line calls to mind the valley of the shadow, and no bell can "toll" without waking the ghost of John Donne. The title, too, splits itself between the here and the hereafter, the literal and the figurative. The cure of souls is one of the offices of Catholic and Anglican priests. It means, literally, *care* of souls—all the day-to-day ministering that priests do for their congregation. Levertov changes "the" to "a," though, and thereby suggests one of those oddities of biological nomenclature like a shrewdness of apes or a crash of rhinos. A cure of souls is this group of people the pastor is shepherding through their fear of death ("fear no evil," as Psalm 23 has it), or perhaps even through death itself, as they are "souls" after all, and there is an eerily permeable solidity to the poem, as if it were ghosted by itself.

Levertov's gift was for a certain subdued urgency. (It's why an immediate and obvious urgency—like the Vietnam War—just crushed her.) A charitable critic would say that Levertov's language is shorn of ornament and refuses to call attention to itself; it is both aerated and animated by the silences in which it claims its own existence. A less charitable critic would say the language is often dull and/or hortatory. At times Levertov rises above both of these readings with forms that seem to merge the mind and its perceptions, as if a very particular world came to life by means of the gaze that was cast upon it. That's not a bad definition of all durable poetry: a world becomes real only as it is realized in *these particular words*:

I have

a line or groove I love
runs down
my body from breastbone
to waist. It speaks of
eagerness, of
distance.

Your long back,
the sand color and
how the bones show, say

what sky after sunset
almost white
over a deep woods to which

rooks are homing, says.

The way the rhymes and near rhymes stitch the perceptions together; the way those perceptions are both discovered and fulfilled by the form ("It speaks of"—then the little abyss while we wait—"eagerness"); the way a consummate articulation includes an irreducible silence, an extreme intimacy, an inevitable "distance"; and, finally, the way the human heart and the heart of matter have something to say to each other: this seems to me a great piece of writing.

Denise was obsessed with form when I knew her, as was I, as is every serious artist I have known. ("All arts are concerned only with form in the end," said Basil Bunting—an overstatement, but still.) Form for her meant attending to the life or spirit or essential being of the object—a flock of sheep/parishioners, the bodies of lovers—to such an intense degree that that life and the energy of inspiration become coextensive. Word and world are, for a moment, one thing, and for Denise the variety and volatility of contemporary life was such that only an exquisitely independent free verse could manage this marriage. The belief is reminiscent of Hopkins's ideas about "inscape," though it never would have occurred to Hopkins to assume that given forms couldn't be expressive in this sense, and it amounts to a metaphysical aesthetic. You have to *believe* that an object or person has some "essential energy," first of all, and, secondly, that language can share it.

We used to sit up in her office in the Stanford English Department and talk about these things. And also about William Wordsworth, an obsession we shared. She loved how the poems reminded her of her childhood in England, and she felt a vivid kinship with Wordsworth's sense of poetic vocation. (She even wrote an essay called "My Prelude" in which she—humorously but sincerely—pledges her fidelity to poetry as a child.) I loved the grand architectonic movements of Wordsworth's long poems, the way you could feel form operating like a spiritual current in the verse, the way you could believe—while godlessly reciting the lines way up in Northern California's transcendent hills, for example—that it *was* a spiritual current, as in these lines from "The Ruined Cottage," which is about a woman whose husband left for a war and never returned:

"I perceive
You look at me, and you have cause. Today
I have been travelling far, and many days
About the fields I wander, knowing this
Only, that what I seek I cannot find.
And so I waste my time: for I am changed;
And to myself," said she, "have done much wrong,
And to this helpless infant. I have slept
Weeping, and weeping I have waked; my tears
Have flow'd as if my body were not such
As others are, and I could never die.
But I am now in mind and in my heart
More easy, and I hope," said she, "that Heaven
Will give me patience to endure the things
Which I behold at home." It would have grieved
Your very soul to see her. Sir, I feel
The story linger in my heart. I fear
'Tis long and tedious, but my spirit clings
To that poor woman: so familiarly
Do I perceive her manner, and her look
And presence, and so deeply do I feel
Her goodness, that not seldom in my walks
A momentary trance comes over me;
And to myself I seem to muse on one
By sorrow laid asleep or borne away,
A human being destined to awake
To human life, or something very near
To human life, when he shall come again
For whom she suffered.

I was trying to write a long poem that brought Wordsworth's meters, and the meaningful sorrow they conveyed, into the twentieth century. I had a well-developed (and well-defended!) critical theory about how this might happen. Denise thought that all forms of art were not only historically determined (inarguable) but bound to the circumstances and politics of their time (arguable). She believed that formal decisions were ultimately political decisions, and that if you understood this dynamic and persisted in using "antiquated" forms, then you were implicitly supporting the cultural values of the time in which those forms emerged or reached their full expressiveness; and if you weren't conscious of this dynamic or didn't believe it, then you could produce at best pastiche, at worst unconscious agitprop. I agreed with the principle behind her notions of organic form (which to some extent derived from Coleridge) but felt that she applied it too inflexibly, and I thought that sensibility and circumstance could enliven a form that had fallen out of fashion. It's dangerous for any poet to become famous for her ideas; it's easier to destroy an achieved style than it is a public persona. In any event, now it seems to me that we were both right: there are too many examples of old forms charged with new life to dispute the entire enterprise. Unfortunately, I didn't write any of them.

We also talked of Seattle, where I had lived and where she had just decided to move. She would be buried five years later in Lake View Cemetery, which was the title of a poem I had written a year earlier when I spent hours every afternoon on long walks going around and around the unspecific nature of the grief I felt and the way it seemed to be behind—the engine of, as it were—every poem I wrote.

> *This is the time of year*
> *the lengthening dark appears*
> *as light in all the trees.*

> *Enameled chestnuts ease*
> *from their skins*
> *and I am holding again*

> *the deep casked color and shape*
> *a low note might take*
> *before becoming its sound.*

Pretty, I can almost hear her saying. Then the wry annihilating little British grin.

The day after Ammons gave his disastrous reading, he squeezed absurdly but cheerfully into a student desk and tried to convince ten un-awed undergraduates of Ralph Waldo Emerson's greatness as a poet. "The Snow-Storm" was the poem he used to make his case, and for almost three decades—until I began following the trail of these notes—all I remembered of the hour was the poignant incongruity of that towering, ungainly, large-spirited man trying to convey with words and gestures the pinpoint specificity of that poem. And all I remembered from that poem was an arresting phrase from its last line, "frolic architecture," which in fact is the ice ax that broke open all these frozen thoughts.

I was in a hotel in New York City, bald and blasted from cancer treatments, addled and exhausted by an interview that left me feeling disquieted by some of the responses I had given about faith and poetry. It wasn't so much the substance of what I had said that unsettled me as the ease with which it had come to my tongue. Chekhov once said that after a writer reads a work to an audience, all he can do is bow smilingly as he backs out of the room. Everything else is extenuation, attenuation, lies. I don't recall whether Chekhov was primarily defending the mystery and autonomy of art or pointing out the uneasy mix of pride and humility inherent in such a calling, but that day in New York, both messages came to mind. I felt that I had been caught standing at a podium past my time, that I was traducing upon mysteries—poetry, faith, love—to which I had been admitted only by a great grace, and which would most certainly vanish the minute they had been "mastered."

I lay down on the bed with a book by the poet Susan Howe, *That This*. It was written in the wake of her husband's sudden death, and I had grabbed a galley off the shelves at *Poetry* magazine (which I was then editing) in an act of . . . grace, maybe, or penance, or both. I had read and respected Howe for years, but I hadn't ever felt any real kinship with her work, and our one meeting had gone badly. In 2004 we were on a panel together at a Wallace Stevens conference in Connecticut. Howe was there because she had written brilliantly on Stevens and was seen to have inherited and extended something of his cerebral yet sensuous style. Sixty-ish, whippet-tense, with a face like a blade and a mind to match, she fended off a gaggle of fans even before we began. I was there solely because I was the new editor of *Poetry* and Stevens had had a long association with the magazine. Solitary, a bit shell-shocked already by the microscopic topics and prodigal jargon (this was my first academic conference), I sat down nervously to wait my turn.

The auditorium was filled to capacity, with many well-known poets and critics in attendance and everyone (or so it seemed to me) rapt in awe as Howe began. Our charge was to speculate on the influence of Stevens's work on American poets in fifty years' time. I don't recall a word Howe said, except that his influence was likely to be much the same—that is, deep and durable for any truly serious poet. I don't remember much of what I said after I became distracted by the little fuse of fury sparking up and down the rows of academics. It leapt the chasm between them and the stage and went sizzling through Massimo Bacigalupo, the esteemed Italian translator and critic who was also on the panel ("Seamus Heaney is *nothing* compared to Stevens," he told me when I expressed my admiration for the former), finally ending in the diminutive but formidable woman who sat visibly trembling three feet from me. Then came the blast.

I have always felt that Stevens's work breaks in half. After the unabashedly Shakespearean extravagance of his first book, *Harmonium*, which he labored over until he was forty-four years old, then the gentler but still more-than-mortal harmonics of his next two books (*Ideas of Order* and roughly half of *The Man with the Blue Guitar*), there comes a plunge. Or not a plunge, exactly, because the level of writing as writing remains high, but something has been leeched out of it—life, you might say. (I'm sure I did say.) "The greatest poverty is not to live in a physical world," Stevens writes in a late poem, as if he were all too aware of the untouchable bubble he'd come to inhabit in long poems of pure abstraction such as "The Auroras of Autumn" or "Notes Toward a Supreme Fiction." From my new perch at *Poetry* magazine, where my in-box was daily flooded by acolytes of precisely this late style, it seemed to me that this bubble had begun to enclose an entire literary culture. There in genteel Connecticut, amid a couple hundred people who had spent noble professional lives immersed in the work of a poet they loved and were there to celebrate, I pulled out my tiny, tiny pin.

Ego is a tricky business in art. It's not at all easy to survive as a poet, even if, maybe especially if, one has acquired all kinds of honors and is professionally secure. There is some necessary psychic pressure, and some profound existential unease, to which the forms of one's art must remain responsive. Many years ago, in the first real essay I ever wrote about poetry, I used the metaphor of form as a diving bell in which the poet descends into an element that would otherwise destroy him. I sensed at the time both the artistic and psychological dangers of that metaphor, that one's forms might become merely protective and not expressive, or that they would eventually be unable to withstand the ever-increasing pressure required for advances in one's art. What I did not realize were the potential practical effects of living out this metaphor: the diving bell that enables one to plumb and survive one's private depths can become, out in the glare of public life, a wrecking ball.

I had been editing *Poetry* for less than a year when I went to that conference in Connecticut, and I had already decided that the job was not for me. I enjoyed the work, actually, but it was overwhelming, and the pull of my own poetry—or, rather, the pressure of the silence in which I seemed to be both sinking and suffocating—was too strong. It was often hard not to feel the concerns and careers of other poets as anything other than a distraction and a nuisance. I suspect that this would have been the case even if a two-hundred-million-dollar bequest from the pharmaceutical heiress Ruth Lilly had not just dropped on the bow of that tiny craft that had puttered along on financial fumes for a century. But suddenly, as Roy Scheider says in *Jaws*, we needed a bigger boat, and we had to build it right in the midst of the storm of expectations, recriminations, and bureaucratic chaos that our good fortune had unleashed.

To say that I was not equipped for this task is comically understated. Not only was I politically naïve in terms of corporate practices and politics, but the habits of thrift acquired in my undergraduate years had, by my mid-thirties, hardened into a physiology. I was a money camel and could cross vast expanses of time with the merest trickle of income. Eventually an entire foundation would emerge around the magazine, with a president who had a background in the business world, a mission statement that I genuinely believed in (to make poetry more a part of American life), and a functioning board. (Though I came to miss the ingrown old-Chicago carnival feel of those early board meetings, in which I might hear about the latest mad-dog chat one member had just had with "Rummy"—Donald Rumsfeld—or the most recent exploits of the intelligent but incontinent pet monkey that ambled around some legendary downtown aerie in a dinner jacket and diapers.) For that first year, though, I was the sad captain of this rich ship, and for me, two hundred million dollars might as well have been two hundred. I still trembled to buy a lamp for my desk.

To me, then, if not to some of my friends and family who felt I'd hit the mother lode, it seemed to make perfect sense that by the time of the Connecticut conference, my wife and I, who had been married for only a month, had already begun talking about making our escape. That Danielle understood and shared this impulse was one of the things that first soldered our souls together. The plan was to spend one more year at *Poetry*, during which time I could stuff my hump with enough money to fuel our first year of freelancing. My starting salary was sixty thousand dollars, after all, which seemed to me positively oligarch-ish. Now I realize I was getting screwed. Money can separate a person from certain aspects of experience just as surely as drugs—and can be even harder to renounce. If I stare long enough, I can just see the selves we were fifteen years ago, lighting out to live on love and poetry.

No doubt we were heavily influenced by Donald Hall, whose famous farmhouse in New Hampshire we first visited on a memorable afternoon during our honeymoon. Don has written extensively about resigning his comfortable teaching position in his mid-forties and moving with Jane Kenyon to his family's old farm, where they both forged a life as independent writers until her death from leukemia in 1995. Danielle and I, too, had just begun to think in concrete terms about our departure, and our plan was to move to the house in Tennessee that had been in her family for generations, which she was just beginning to write about in poems and prose. The similarities flattered all of us, and we played them up—at least until, just three weeks before the date we had determined that I would formally resign, I got the diagnosis that has determined everything since. Suddenly the symmetry between our lives and Don's seemed even more apparent, and more malign.

But all that lay ahead of me that afternoon in Connecticut when I found myself suddenly confronted by a blunt crowd with a sharp weapon: Susan Howe. I had tried to backtrack ("*Half* of Stevens is sublime . . .") but somehow found myself only making things worse (". . . just not the half you think"). The crowd fed her leading questions and cheers, and she fed me to the crowd: *Poetry* was moribund and I was a dinosaur. I wouldn't recognize the truly new in art if it bit me in my hegemonic ass. The only emperor is the emperor of ice cream.

I had never intended to be so provocative. I thought, if anything, that my reading of Stevens was too obvious, but it was as if I had called him a pedophile. No doubt the reaction stemmed as much from my manner and tone—the manner and tone of a man already on his way out—as from what I said. When it was over, I asked a friend—my only one!—if I had come across as arrogant, and she said she knew of a wonderful little restaurant we should try. I thought I could brave the aftermath and crept cautiously into the cocktail party after the talk, but the backs turned, and the cliques clacked, and my handlers ended up bundling me out of the conference under cover of darkness as if I were fleeing East Berlin.

Nine years later in New York, reeling from treatments, turning as ever to poetry for both refuge and release, I opened Howe's book of elliptical sympathies and extreme grief and found her trying to salvage meaning from the same ancient source.

Nietzsche says that for Heraclitus all contradictions run into harmony, even if they are invisible to the human eye. Lyric is transparent—as hard to see as black or glare ice. The paved roadway underneath is our search for aesthetic truth. Poetry, false in the tricks of its music, draws harmony from necessity and random play. In this aggressive age of science, sound-colored secrets, unperceivable in themselves, can act as proof against our fear of emptiness.

I read this passage over and over. (It is itself darkly transparent.) It still seems to me a fresh and useful description of what poetry ("sound-colored secrets") can do and why we read and need it ("proof against our fear of emptiness"). It is also a beautiful—and, I think, accurate—description of what an experience of God can be and do in our lives. Instead of the paved roadway being our search for *aesthetic* truth, though— of what value would that be, finally? can there even be aesthetic truth without some other, more ultimate truth as precedent?—I would say that the road is our search for *spiritual* truth. This is why a poet's technical decisions are moral decisions, why matters of form and sound have existential meaning and consequences. It's also why poetry is so important in the world, even if few people read it. Its truth is irreducible, inexhaustible, atomic; its existence as natural and necessary as a stand of old-growth trees so far in the Arctic that only an oil company would ever see it; and just like those threatened trees, its reality ramifies into the lives of people for whom it remains utterly irrelevant and/or obscure. The same may be said for other arcane ways of facing God. "Sorrows have been passed," as Howe concludes in that passage above, "and unknown continents approached."

After reading this sentence in that lonely hotel room in

New York where I felt unsure of my life in poetry—and unsure of my life at all—I tracked down Howe's e-mail address and wrote her a letter of admiration and apology and, when a few hours later I received her warm reply, felt a circle close inside of me and outside of time.

have not lost the thread. That Howe quote comes from a section in her book titled "Frolic Architecture," which recalled Emerson to me, which recalled Ammons, which led me to pick up his notebooks in the middle of the night, which set me on this quest to figure out what it is, exactly, we want when we can't stop wanting. Ammons was drawn to Emerson because of the creedless transcendentalism, the natural supernaturalism that was not only accessible to every individual but also accessible *only* to the individual. Looked at negatively, "The Snow-Storm," like much of Emerson's writing, delivers a clean whiff of metaphysics without any stench of real content. Looked at positively—again, like much of Emerson—it's a prophetic articulation of a spiritual impulse that has come to full fruition in modern times, one that is determined to reconcile a deep intuition of otherness with the adamantine materialism that both science and our clock-logic lives seem to confirm. A frolic architecture, you could call it.

> *Come see the north wind's masonry.*
> *Out of an unseen quarry evermore*
> *Furnished with tile, the fierce artificer*
> *Curves his white bastions with projected roof*

Round every windward stake, or tree, or door.
Speeding, the myriad-handed, his wild work
So fanciful, so savage, nought cares he
For number or proportion. Mockingly,
On coop or kennel he hangs Parian wreaths;
A swan-like form invests the hidden thorn;
Fills up the farmer's lane from wall to wall,
Maugre the farmer's sighs; and, at the gate,
A tapering turret overtops the work.
And when his hours are numbered, and the world
Is all his own, retiring, as he were not,
Leaves, when the sun appears, astonished Art
To mimic in slow structures, stone by stone,
Built in an age, the mad wind's night-work,
The frolic architecture of the snow.

To see this scene, you have to hear it first: the way sound
sleeves or "invests" sense (note, for example, how the *form* the
snow makes echoes the *thorn* it covers); the finical excess ("A
tapering turret overtops the work"); the syntactical delibera-
tion especially of the end, which comes to a close with a line
that feels as ridged and turreted as the scene it describes: "The
frolic architecture of the snow." The form of this poem is at
odds with its content. The former is all painstaking care; the
latter is savage havoc. (Now *this* is an old form—blank verse—
animated by a new imagination.) The effect is to marry the
autonomous activity of individual creation (the frolic) with
blind necessity (the architecture), without violating the integ-
rity of either. Whether the revelation happened in nature or

in language doesn't really matter. What matters is that it happened in time.

> *Space opens and from the heart of the matter*
> *sheds a descending grace that makes,*
> *for a moment, that naked thing, Being,*
> *a thing to understand.*

—NORMAN MacCAIG

But is that enough? These moments of grace and inspiration, of nature and art, are they enough to hang faith on? And faith in what, exactly? I am drawn to Ammons because he is drawn to a life beyond his own, but in fact Ammons had little patience with "institutional" religion and could be particularly caustic about Christianity, the religion of his childhood. His poems record an intense but indeterminate devotion, are the testaments of a man who wouldn't believe in anything at all beyond the material world were it not for the insights he has been given in his own life and poetry, yet by means of the insights—these "spots of time," as Wordsworth called them—it becomes possible to live, even to praise. In a 1955 letter to the poet Josephine Miles, Ammons writes:

> Which is to say I am a mystic—but by memory only. For an instant, about ten years ago, I *felt* the perspective from space to earth. Sick as I may have been, I was *there*. By the use of the intelligence, of course, you can work up such perspectives at will, but it's a very different thing from *being* there—in the mixture of joy and of a sort of mad sorrow at the lot of man. What I seemed to see has remained literally the weight of the world. All the good realists, materialists and rationalists I've

been able to get my hands on have done nothing to that experience. Perhaps only an equally powerful experience, certainly stronger than intellectual conviction, in another direction can ever move me.

The great Jewish theologian Abraham Joshua Heschel once defined faith as primarily faithfulness to a time when we had faith. We remember these moments of heightened awareness in our lives, these clearings within consciousness in which faith is self-evident and God too obvious and omnipresent to need that name, and we try to remain true to them. It's a tenuous, tenacious discipline of memory and hope.

Some Christian theologians have seen their practice similarly. Karl Barth begins his massive *Church Dogmatics* by saying that theology "knows the light which is intrinsically perfect and reveals everything in a flash. Yet it knows it only in the prism of this act, which, however radically or existentially it may be understood, is still a human act." Barth goes on to talk about how limited this act is, and how distinct theology (like any human endeavor) is from divine revelation. For Barth, that means Scripture and, more specifically, the person of Jesus Christ as revealed in the Gospels.

It goes without saying that few modern poets would draw this distinction. The inspiration they are given in a work of art is revelation in the Barthian sense (if they even believe in this kind of transcendent revelation), and they will burn in hell—the hell of mediocrity, at the very least—if they don't trust it. And trust it, in fact, *more* than what is handed down to them as "divine" revelation. Occasionally someone will contest this notion or will raise the question of whether all inspiration is necessarily benign. Gerard Manley Hopkins famously renounced poetry for seven years because it "was not consistent with his vocation" as a priest. Franz Kafka, after a rare spell of inspired composition during the night, wrote in a letter to Max Brod the following morning:

> Writing is a sweet and wonderful reward, but for what? In the night it became clear to me, as clear as a child's lesson book, that it is the reward for serving the devil.

That puts a rather different spin on the old poetry-is-prayer argument so beloved by contemporary poets. Everyone is always claiming that their inspiration came from "somewhere else," and everyone wants more than anything to be released again into those inexplicable currents in which existence becomes "a thing to understand." But what if the thing to understand is that there is no thing to understand? What if at the heart of creation there is only a void, or even some active malevolence?

> *Understand that it can drink till it is*
> *sick, but cannot drink till it is satisfied.*

> *It alone knows you. It does not wish you well.*

> *Understand that when your mother, in her only*
> *pregnancy, gave birth to twins*

painfully stitched into the flesh, the bone of one child

was the impossible-to-remove cloak that confers
invisibility. The cloak that maimed it gave it power.

Painfully stitched into the flesh, the bone of the other child

was the impossible-to-remove cloak that confers
visibility. The cloak that maimed it gave it power.

Envying the other, of course each twin

tried to punish and become the other.
Understand that when the beast within you

succeeds again in paralyzing into unending

incompletion whatever you again had the temerity to
try to make

its triumph is made sweeter by confirmation of its

rectitude. It knows that it alone
knows you. It alone remembers your mother's

mother's grasping immigrant bewildered

stroke-filled slide-to-the-grave
you wiped from your adolescent American feet.

Your hick purer-than-thou overreaching veiling

mediocrity. Understand that you can delude others but
not what you more and more

now call the beast within you. Understand

the cloak that maimed each gave each power.
Understand that there is a beast within you

that can drink till it is

sick, but cannot drink till it is satisfied. Understand
that it will use the conventions of the visible world

to turn your tongue to stone. It alone

knows you. It does
not wish you well. These are instructions for the wrangler.

This poem by Frank Bidart has a mesmerizing, modern Delphic quality to it. I remember first coming across it when I was reading manuscripts one weekend afternoon in my high-rise short-term sublet—this is when I was sure I was leaving—in downtown Chicago and stopping to stare out at the sharply modern winter cityscape that suddenly seemed like a gleam of demon teeth. And l loved it.

Yet I'm not sure if the poem isn't something only an artist would respond to. A particular kind of artist, too, not simply one whose "cloak that maimed it gave it power"—which is probably true to some extent for all committed artists—but one who had embraced a truth he was meant to resist, or to perceive only glancingly. There are such truths. When Simone Weil says, "The mutual love of God and man is suffering," she is uttering one. Indeed, the key to reading a writer like Weil is much the same as the key to reading poetry. You can't let the flashes of insight harden into "knowledge." You have to remain true to those moments of truth. (Weil means to emphasize the fallen nature of reality, wherein "Absence is the form God's presence takes in this world.") Scripture itself often demands just this sort of indirect perception. I am moved by the moment in Exodus when, according to the King James Version, after Moses demands some sign that God is real, God tells him to stand aside so that he can see God's "back parts." It's comical—I imagine God giving a little sashay—and obviously metaphorical. But it's also profound, revealing a truth that, in this world, can never be fully revealed.

MOMENTARY

I never glimpse her but she goes
Who had been basking in the sun,
Her links of chain mail one by one
Aglint with pewter, bronze and rose.

I never see her lying coiled
Atop the garden step, or under

A dark leaf, unless I blunder
And by some motion she is foiled.

Too late I notice as she passes
Zither of chromatic scale—
I only ever see her tail
Quicksilver into tall grasses.

I know her only by her flowing,
By her glamour disappearing
Into shadow as I'm nearing—
I only recognize her going.

—A. E. STALLINGS

This poem—which I also read in manuscript for *Poetry*, but this time in the basement of a house, a *home*, on the north side of Chicago, the mad patter of twin little two-year-olds audible from above—seems to me to describe a much-saner relation to one's art (and by extension one's consciousness, and by grace one's god) than does the poem by Bidart. The relation is by no means entirely *safe*: the controlling metaphor of "Momentary" is a snake, after all. But the energy and aim of the poem is quite different, aimed outward rather than inward, and suggesting that it's not simply that the hunger that gives rise to art must be greater than what art can satisfy. The hunger must be *other* than what art can satisfy. The poem is means, not end. When art becomes the latter, it eventually acquires an autonomous hunger of its own, and "it does not wish you well."

Hunger for *what*, though? ("Ah, the old questions, the old answers," says droll, doomed Hamm in *Endgame*. "There's nothing like them!") One obvious answer is God—the end, in both senses of that word, of all human longing. One devious answer is death—"an urge inherent in all organic life to restore an earlier state of things," as Freud put it. One fashionable answer is that there is no answer: it's all just nature, genes rotely ramming home their mechanical codes one by one. We want because dissatisfaction equals survival: we are designed to improve and impart our hunger, breeding descendants with ever-keener teeth.

If we are conscious and honest, each of these answers will likely seem right at various times of our lives. If we are conscious and honest, each of them, at another time, will seem wrong.

As I have worked on this book, which seems to feed equally on memory and oblivion, vitality and futility, I have thought repeatedly of this quote from the theoretical physicist and sometime theologian John Polkinghorne:

> What gives continuity are not the atoms themselves but the almost infinitely complex information-bearing pattern in which they are organized. The essence of

this pattern is the soul. It will dissolve at death with the decay of the body, but it is a perfectly coherent belief that the faithful God will not allow it to be lost but will preserve it in the divine memory.

That we might be remembered: what an almost impossible thought that is. That there is a consciousness capacious enough, merciful enough, to recall each of us in our entireties just as we recall our own fragile but all-meaningful moments. That our lives might be the Lord's insight.

Dietrich Bonhoeffer, just before his execution by the Nazis in 1945, exhibited a bravery at once so bracing and daunting that one wants to find a chink in it. There isn't one. Or there is only one: "I want my life," he writes in a poem from that time. "I demand my / own life back. My past. You!" This is not what one expects from a man confronting his own death. It's not the future that Bonhoeffer feels slipping from him, but the past; not some totality of existence he fears losing—he still believes in salvation—but its molecular singularity, all the minute perceptions and sensations, retained by the body if not the mind, that comprise one particular human consciousness. This is an abstract articulation of a reality that is gloriously, excruciatingly concrete. What is it we want when we can't stop wanting? "Lord," prays a character in Ilya Kaminsky's *Dancing in Odessa*, "give us what you have already given."

I BECAME EDITOR of *Poetry* in the summer of 2003, and the first official event over which I presided was a long-standing

Chicago tradition called Poetry Day, which that year culminated with a large public reading by Mary Oliver. This was a challenge. Not only had Oliver been invited before I came on board, but also, just a few years earlier, I had written, for the very pages of *Poetry*, a blistering review of her latest book—which, thank God, the editors had declined to publish.

One of the great things about editing, though, is that it teaches you to read *toward* enthusiasm. This is not necessarily the best stance for a critic, whose praise, if it's going to have any authority and credibility at all, should be rare and hardwon. And a too-instant enthusiasm can be lethal for a young poet, who needs honest antipathies to sharpen the gift that her sympathies enlarge. An editor, though, especially one responsible for a monthly magazine, and *especially* one whose literary predispositions are, let us say, snarlish, quickly discovers that if complete critical approval is the only criterion for inclusion, then either he or the magazine is going under.

I became a different kind of reader. I spent my first three months at *Poetry* reading through a year's worth of unread manuscripts that had accumulated because of the international publicity that the Ruth Lilly gift had caused and the demands that publicity had placed on the tiny staff. Bankers boxes were piled floor to ceiling in the basement room of the Newberry Library, where the magazine then had its offices. It was in those early months that I began to develop Sisyphean powers of persistence that enabled me to trawl through manuscripts for eight hours at a stretch. Learning to do this taught me something not only about my own limitations— it's tough to hold on to your one little aesthetic umbrella amid a storm of styles—but about survival. And not only of poems.

I started out as a poet believing that greatness will out, as it were, that fate will find and save the masterpieces from oblivion no matter what. A decade of standing in that afore-mentioned storm, as well as making my way through the collected works of just about every American poet of note for the annual Ruth Lilly Prize for lifetime achievement, has convinced me otherwise. Chance and power play a large part, and I feel sure that some genuinely great things fall through the cracks—forever. But even aside from that, there are many, many poems that, though the future will likely find them cold and curiously dark, can nevertheless light the time we're in. This is a sadness, yes, but also a freedom. Take your eyes off eternity's horizon and you might miss the meteor that flashes by every century or so (though I doubt it), but the immedi-ate landscape is suddenly much more interesting. There is a spiritual lesson here.

I can't say I had learned that lesson by the time I met Mary Oliver, but I was primed for it. What I had objected to in my review of her most recent book was a certain transactional element in her relationship with the natural world. The poet goes out for a walk and gets a daily dose of awe, as if nature were an epiphany machine. It ought to be harder than this, I had thought to myself. And then, as I worked my way back-ward through all her work, it suddenly was: a poem midway through *American Primitive* about an eerie owl striking some hapless and never-named creature. It was spare and unsparing, wholly alert and disquietingly narcotic at the same time. I read it over and over. I practically had it memorized by the time I left the office promptly at five, a clerk of verse, and with the deathless prose of my first official introduction tucked carefully in my coat pocket, headed out to meet the most famous poet in the country.

Famous poet. Hard even to utter the phrase without irony. "It's like being famous in your family," Mark Strand once said in response to an awestruck interviewer wondering what the life was like. Strand meant to mock the whole notion of a poet being famous, at least with regard to "real" fame, at least in manic modern America with its ten billion screaming screens. But between the ingenuous question and the ironized answer lies a complicated truth.

American poets may pay lip service to old ideas of literary fame—"that last infirmity of noble mind," as Milton said—and some may even aspire to it, but the word has become too corrupted to refer to that ambition. Fame is the common currency of American cultural life, even among people and institutions who profess to have scorn for it. A poet can pretend not to be affected by this, which is what Strand—a Pulitzer Prize winner, tall as Gregory Peck and just as chiseled—was doing. But really no one is immune. Those who feel cheated of fame become predictably embittered. Those granted some measure of fame can either reconcile themselves to the reality of being a poet in modern America, taking some consolation perhaps in the fundamental incommensurability between the furious spirit that is the source of the poems and the frivolous energy that attaches to the poet. Or they can go all in with readings and social media mania and Q&As about "what it's like," all the while accumulating something that is not really there. It is the dream of fame, the fumes of fame, which can come to enclose a "public poet" with an invisible but impenetrable nimbus.

Not Mary Oliver. I first saw her in the lobby of her downtown hotel, dressed for this upscale occasion in hiking boots, wrinkled chinos, and what appeared to be a hunting jacket a size too large. It looked like she might have cut her own hair. Her head was bent over a thick book that I saw, as she rose, was *The Faerie Queene*. My face must have registered some surprise. "I'm not young," she said, shrugging as she opened her knapsack and exchanged Edmund Spenser for a pack of cigarettes. "I want to spend what time I have left with masterpieces." She meant it, too. I'd see her reading that massive sixteenth-century poem two other times during the evening, once when sitting right beside me while waiting to go onstage. It didn't occur to me to be offended. By that point I was in awe.

And, I should say, in love. My wife, who was not then my wife but only a woman I had known for three gloriously disordered months, was sitting somewhere behind me in that auditorium. I could feel her presence just as surely as I had felt it that morning when—at the break of dawn, sublimely and purifyingly naked—she had spread her arms out wide in front of the floor-to-ceiling windows in my anonymous sublet and shouted, "It's Poetry Day, Chicago!" If I hadn't fallen in love with her the instant we first met, I certainly had a few weeks later when I ran into her ("ran into her," as if all my errands hadn't suddenly necessitated trips into her neighborhood) at a bookstore where, on a Saturday night, she sat alone with a huge *Riverside Shakespeare* spread out in front of her, all her lovely attention given over to ruined Lear. I was a goner then, though for months we kept the relationship a secret because we worked together, and even I in my organizational innocence knew the dynamic was not ideal. I suspect the atmospheric pressure was apparent to anyone paying attention.

And Mary Oliver pays attention. Realizing that, from this distance, makes me wince a bit. Danielle was waiting outside the hotel when I emerged with Mary. Mary was traveling alone because Molly, her partner for more than forty years, was already sick with the illness that would kill her. Not that Mary mentioned any of this to us. I don't know whether she was living in that initial period of obstinate, desperate disregard to which every cancer victim or caretaker seems to have recourse, or whether it was simply her nature. But she gave little hint of the catastrophe—and it must surely have felt, after four decades of what was obviously a great love, like catastrophe—that loomed. We talked of Spenser and Emerson, of poetry and *Poetry*. I walked in distracted bliss, occasionally feeling the electric current when I brushed up against Danielle, occasionally fingering the minuscule bump that had recently appeared just above my clavicle, so tiny and mercurial that half the time I couldn't find it.

Somewhere along crowded Michigan Avenue Mary suddenly stopped and picked up a piece of meat. At least that's what I thought at first. When she spread the gray-red mess out on her hands, you could see that it was, or at least had been, a bird. A pigeon, in fact, which she proceeded to describe with avid eyes and intelligent touch, showing us exactly where the hawk had struck, the talons clutched and torn. Most likely, she said, the hawk had dropped this half-eaten carcass into a crowd from which no recovery was possible, but all I could think of—or am I projecting this backwards?—was a fate falling so hard that it split an existence right in two. We stood there for a moment, huddled around the half carcass in Mary's hands, until I gently suggested we had to go. "Okay," Mary said. Then she stuck the bloody bird in the pocket of her jacket and walked on.

I recall little of the reading (and nothing of my introduction—not so deathless after all). There have been so many of them by now. I myself have stood in front of countless audiences and heard poems that once came as mysteries pour forth as performance. It's not a lie, this performance. Crucial human communication and consolation can occur in these exchanges. But it's not *not* a lie, either. The self that intones the poem is not the soul that received it. One needs to know the difference. I suspect that Mary Oliver, up there in front of eight hundred people with half a dead pigeon in her pocket, did. Maybe that was the very reason she held on to that thing, to both recall and forestall the reality that was forcing itself upon her. And I do know she held on to it, because at the party after the reading, which took place in one of the black, classic Mies van der Rohe towers that make it seem as if you're floating out over Lakeshore Drive, we both sought refuge in the kitchen at the same time. The first thing she did was to pull that apotropaic pigeon out to show me—to show us both?—that it was still there.

THE SENSE OF MORTALITY—our own, of course, but also that of those we most love—doesn't only cast us backward. It also propels imagination forward. It makes us imagine heavens in which wounds are healed and losses restored, or helps us to ameliorate oblivions by imagining our atoms alive in other forms. But heaven too often turns out to be little more than projections of the precious self ad infinitum, and it is cold comfort to think of one's dear smithereens blasted throughout some new forms of matter from which we—whatever it is that makes us, us—have vanished. Here's Polkinghorne again:

> Death is present in this world because of the second law of thermodynamics, which says that in the end, disorder always wins over order. However, it seems perfectly coherent to believe that God could bring into being a new kind of "matter" with such strong self-organizing principles that the drift to disorder would no longer happen.

Or perhaps: that the notion of disorder would be naïve? That we might be a form, or part of a form, whose fruition, for now, we can intuit but not inhabit—that heaven and oblivion might have one name, which every poet, in one way or another, is trying to speak.

WHITE OWL FLIES INTO AND OUT OF THE FIELD

Coming down out of the freezing sky
with its depths of light,

like an angel, or a Buddha with wings,

it was beautiful, and accurate,

striking the snow and whatever was there

with a force that left the imprint

of the tips of its wings—five feet apart—

and the grabbing thrust of its feet,

and the indentation of what had been running

through the white valleys of the snow—

and then it rose, gracefully,

and flew back to the frozen marshes

to lurk there, like a little lighthouse,

in the blue shadows—

so I thought:

maybe death isn't darkness, after all,

but so much light wrapping itself around us—

as soft as feathers—

that we are instantly weary of looking, and looking,

and shut our eyes, not without amazement,

and let ourselves be carried,

as through the translucence of mica,

to the river that is without the least dapple or shadow,

that is nothing but light—scalding, aortal light—

in which we are washed and washed

out of our bones.

—MARY OLIVER

A hard, bright clarity, taut and immediate. The highest simplicity without slackness. This coupled with the freest imagination. That's the style I want: a barren beauty, none the less beautiful for its barrenness.

That's Ammons in 1955, reading Jacques Maritain's *Creative Intuition in Art and Poetry* and trying to clarify the radical impersonality and existential intimacy of the "I" in his poems. Trying, that is, to understand how language can sound at once one's deepest self and the larger reality from which that self takes its existence and to which it will inevitably return. To assert and to assent in one gesture. Ammons sought a tone at once so attached to concrete reality, yet so abstracted from any particular consciousness, that it might almost be nature itself talking. (Sometimes it *was* nature talking: "the cedar-cone said you have been ground / down into and whirled.") This "hard, bright clarity" was not, for him, impersonation or projection, but rather a radical revelation of an original truth, *the* original truth, actually, which is that we are one with everything around us, which means that subjective imagination and objective reality are expressions of each other. "Are we to think," asks Maritain, "that in such an experience, creative in nature, Things are grasped in the Self and the Self is grasped in Things, and subjectivity becomes a means of catching obscurely the inner side of Things?"

If man and matter share some form of life, then surely they share some form of death as well. This is the possibility hinted at by the ends of the Gilbert (page 7) and Oliver (page 49) poems, both of which conjure a spiritual reality that they simultaneously deny. The spiritual feeling of each poem is quite different, though. It's one thing to leave a "greed tough as winter," which is to insist on some final resistance to the natural forces that are removing one from existence. (Though everything else in Gilbert's poem does suggest a calm acquiescence.) It's another thing to imagine being able actually to release oneself into those currents. (Though it's worth keeping in mind that the lucky, light-wrapped rodent—if that's even what it is; the anonymity is important—in Oliver's poem is being eaten alive.) Still, both poems fit well enough into the metaphysical materialism that derives from Emerson and was so beloved by Ammons. Ammons, though, sometimes filled in his moments of faith with a little more content.

> I know if I find you I will have to leave the earth
> and go on out
>   over the sea marshes and the brant in bays
> and over the hills of tall hickory
> and over the crater lakes and canyons
> and on up through the spheres of diminishing air
> past the blackset noctilucent clouds
>   where one wants to stop and look
> way past all the light diffusions and bombardments

up farther than the loss of sight
    into the unseasonal undifferentiated empty stark

And I know if I find you I will have to stay with the earth
inspecting with thin tools and ground eyes
trusting the microvilli sporangia and simplest
    coelenterates
and praying for a nerve cell
with all the soul of my chemical reactions
and going right on down where the eye sees only traces

You are everywhere partial and entire
You are on the inside of everything and on the outside

I walk down the path down the hill where the sweetgum
has begun to ooze spring sap at the cut
and I see how the bark cracks and winds like no other bark
chasmal to my ant-soul running up and down
and if I find you I must go out deep into your
    far resolutions
and if I find you I must stay here with the separate leaves

This poem is called "Hymn," but you hardly need that prompt in order to assume that the "you" is God, especially since the poem's theology—God is absolutely immanent and absolutely transcendent—is right on the surface and comes straight out of Thomas Aquinas. This poem is about life, but from its first line—"I know if I find you I will have to leave the earth"—it's apparent that the poem is also very much about death. If you are to find life, the poem suggests, you must find God. (I love how that word *stark* either loses its normal grammatical function and becomes a noun, or, even better, is left as an adjective with nothing—or nothing that language can reach—to modify.) If you are to find God, the poem also suggests, you must die. There's no religious paradox here. "When Christ calls a man, he bids him come and die," wrote Bonhoeffer famously, who was echoing Christ himself, who in all three of the synoptic Gospels says that salvation lies in, and only in, loss.

What is a paradox, however, is that "Hymn" is a moving invocation and celebration of God written by a poet who, in his prose, professes not to believe in God. "Hymn" is more explicit about its spiritual lineage than the poems by Oliver and Gilbert, but they all partake of a common tendency among modern artists: the art contains and expresses a faith that the artist, in the rest of his waking life, rejects. And quite often, as in "Hymn," the art relies on, even while extending, the religious language for which the artist has no practical use and of which he is perhaps even contemptuous. Is this a failure of art, then, since presumably a living poem ought not to rely on language that is dead at the root? Or is it a triumph of God, resurrecting blossoms from a branch that seemed irrevocably withered? If the former, how does one change one's art? If the latter, how does one change one's life?

C. K. WILLIAMS—Charlie, his friends called him—won the Ruth Lilly Prize in 2005. This was my second year at *Poetry,* just when Danielle and I were plotting our imminent escape. That summer in Tennessee, in fact, she and I had walked that property where, after her father died in her infancy, she had spent every summer of her life and where we were planning to move, a two-centuries-old tavern-turned-house where two centuries of nobles-turned-soldiers had sat on the porch musing on whatever war they'd lately escaped. The great wave of poems that would result in Danielle's first book had not yet crested, but I could feel it building in her. It was the first summer of our love and the last summer of our innocence, and looking back, I see us moving through those rooms as through an atmosphere of glass, the past so immanent in objects that it seemed as if the right touch, or maybe the wrong one, would release it into immediate being again.

IN ORDER

I've filled my lungs with fog.
I have sobbed in certain, familiar attics
where each fond object had been
hung or shoved away by hands
whose roughness I had loved,
and the carpet smelled of beloved dogs.

Now that that grief's gone and others come
I come back again to understand
the first one, plum blossoms brushing
the attic window as I look out upon

a yard that has been left untended
by any hand but that of God.

—DANIELLE CHAPMAN

The Lilly prize ceremony for Charlie was, as always, an elaborate and money-studded affair, and I'm sure I was well prepared for my part in it because I always am, because I have required great order in my habits to counteract the great disorder in my mind. Yet every single bit of that evening has been lost to me—or perhaps concentrated, distilled, and thereby more deeply discovered—in something that happened as Charlie and I walked up to that same private room for the celebratory dinner. Midway up the stairs he turned and told me eagerly that I had married (as I had!—among ten people in an apartment, and me so joyfully manic that I went for two runs beforehand) a "true beauty." There was no leer in it, no unpleasant power dynamic being tested, no detached and flexing appraisal with which some men sniff women like wine. There was nothing untoward at all. Charlie seemed happy in his own life and love, and he seemed to recognize a similar chance at light in me. I say "chance at light" because—though I must have been glowing, though he too with his hundred-thousand-dollar prize in his pocket must surely have been glowing—I'm sure he was also recognizing and responding to a certain kindred disposition toward darkness.

A year passed. Danielle and I chatted with Donald Hall and his new love, Linda Kunhardt, at a literary gathering at the White House, an event that would have been stiff and miserable and just *wrong* even if I had not been diagnosed with cancer two months earlier. (Adrienne Rich: "Art means nothing if it simply decorates the dinner table of the power which holds it hostage.") Richard Wilbur, in town for a reading and anxious to get back to his dying wife, looked out of a cab window and said, "We've had over fifty years together. We have been so blessed." Danielle emerged excitedly from her study one morning with the poem that is printed above, which she said had just come to her all at once, and which all at once released its sonic shot of sorrow and saving love right into my own nerves. Iraq exploded.

Charlie and I met for lunch down in Hyde Park before his event at the University of Chicago. I forget the exact date, but it must have been relatively close to my diagnosis because I had not yet learned the tactics of expression and deflection that every cancer patient eventually internalizes. Really, there ought to be some sort of standardized guide available so that people don't automatically ask with that lowered tone and those mining eyes *How's your health?* and thereby wrench death right into the room. It is *hard* learning to live "one hour higher than the torments" (Tomas Tranströmer), and I can't tell you the number of times I have missed ten minutes of a conversation while wrestling with a specter I thought I'd managed to subdue. By the same token, there ought to be a whole course given to the newly diagnosed to teach them how little the world wants to hear any real answer to that question, and how intensely they may come to regret the moments when their private panic leaks into their public lives.

I told Charlie too much for us to recover some social equilibrium, too little for any genuine intimacy to develop. We talked of poetry the rest of the time. Or rather of "poetry," since it can be deflecting cocktail fodder as much as the weather. Somewhere in the mess of myself I thought of the poem that represented Charlie's work for me, the strange, sinuous single sentence I first read in my early twenties in Seattle, when I was so determined to be an artist, and so sure of the link between art and suffering, that I set out psychic battlements to fend off any hostile incursions of happiness.

REPRESSION

More and more lately, as, not even minding the slippages yet, the
aches and sad softenings,
I settle into my other years, I notice how many of what I once
thought were evidences of repression,
sexual or otherwise, now seem, in other people anyway, to be
varieties of dignity, withholding, tact,
and sometimes even in myself, certain patiences I would have
once called lassitude, indifference,
now seem possibly to be if not the rewards then at least the
unsuspected, undreamed-of conclusions
to many of the even-then-preposterous self-evolved disciplines,
rigors, almost mortifications
I inflicted on myself in my starting-out days, improvement days,
days when the idea alone of psychic peace,
of intellectual, of emotional quiet, the merest hint, would have
meant inconceivable capitulation.

"Dignity, withholding, tact"—it's obvious enough why the poem occurred to me at that moment, though the place from which it welled up, and the psychological tangle it retightened, were old. The poem is particularly powerful not simply because, with all its kinked clauses, it enacts the repression it describes (I think of a python swallowing a goat), but because, with its syntactical delays and eventual resolution, it offers a kind of relief. But its chief tension between a regret for lost intensity and a genuinely evolved wisdom is never entirely dissipated. I have always thought of Charlie's lines alongside these from Robert Penn Warren:

> We wonder, even as we consider the virtue:
> What is wisdom and what the dimming of faculty?
> What kindliness, and what the guttering of desire?
> What philosophic wisdom, and what the fatigue of the relaxed
> nerve?

Not that I said any of this to Charlie. Not that I even realized any of it at the time. No, we nibbled our salads and sipped our tea, we skimmed our scalding callings until it was time for him to go and perform his own, an event I had planned to attend but suddenly couldn't, it seemed, too much work, too much to catch up on, too much, too much.

Seven years passed. Danielle and I had breakfast with Don and Linda in Vancouver, New Hampshire, Chicago, London. Fanny Howe, Susan's sister, and a writer who as much as any living artist has nourished and fortified my sense of what a genuine faith might look like to a genuinely modern mind, told me over a beer in Michigan that she could wake up an atheist and go to bed a believer, and vice versa, and—her little silver salvaging laugh—*pretty much every goddamn day!* Geoffrey Hill, who before his death in 2016 many critics believed to be the best living English poet, in response to the difficulty we were having getting his work to a critic in 2006, sighed and said, "I guess things are even worse for me than I realized." The Poetry Foundation built a severely beautiful high modernist home for *Poetry*, and on the day it opened Billy Collins and I looked out over the gleam and bling and he said, "Kind of low on the funk factor, wouldn't you say?" I had a bone marrow transplant.

It was around that time—a haze of hospital rooms, pain drugs, rage—that I had my last exchange with Charlie. Because of my wrecked immune system I couldn't leave the house, but I was back at work. In truth I had hardly ever stopped, reading manuscripts and correcting galleys even in the hospital. Among these were galleys for a collection of Charlie's essays, *In Time*, which would be published in 2012, just three years before he would die of leukemia. How many times have I sat talking of cancer with some hale and sympathetic soul whom cancer would end up killing first?

(And suddenly I think of that apogee of elegance, Bill Drenttel, who redesigned *Poetry* in 2005 and was the art director thereafter; who when he first heard that I was sick wrote me a bracing and pity-free e-mail in which he mostly wanted it known that I was not his client or colleague, but his *friend*; and whom I last saw in a sad hospice agonizing over the word for the tool they'd used back in his Minnesota childhood to bore through the eye and thereby end the excruciations of the just-caught fish. I went home and looked it up but before I saw him again the tumor that had turned that fine brain into a carnival of indecipherable outbursts and unnerving animal hunger had shut the whole show down. *Iky stick*.)

I took one of Charlie's essays for the magazine. It speculated on art from cave drawings to contemporary poetry and wondered if we had invented gods not because we fear death, but because we had made works that warranted them. We needed an audience fit for our accomplishments, our augured tigers and auspicious arrows, our fears and wonders, our art. It's an ingenious idea, and related to the more familiar one of the perfections, or near perfections, of art implying or calling forth the other that is their source and goal. (Michelangelo's "The true work of art is but a shadow of the divine perfection" is a famous example.) But there is a world of difference between these two perspectives. Once, in the other order our best creations conjured, we sensed a mystery that enlarged our existence. Now we reach for an explanation and secure a despair. For that's what it is, to lower one's god to the level of one's need, to be the wizard of one's own Oz: despair.

The essay we published was not in fact the one that pierced me. Pierced the poet in me, I should say. The editor in me found the latter essay, which bounced between Philip Larkin and George Herbert, artistic drive and existential meaning, too diffuse. That was Charlie's great weakness as a writer: words.

As I said at the outset of this book, every writer fights the final silence in his own way. It's not really ironic that Charlie, who in the last ten years of his life published ten books, praised Larkin, a writer who for the last decade of his own life lapsed into a silence so absolute that only one real poem trickled out. They were both fighting, in different ways, one war.

AUBADE

I work all day, and get half-drunk at night.
Waking at four to soundless dark, I stare.
In time the curtain-edges will grow light.
Till then I see what's really always there:
Unresting death, a whole day nearer now,
Making all thought impossible but how
And where and when I shall myself die.
Arid interrogation: yet the dread
Of dying, and being dead,
Flashes afresh to hold and horrify.

The mind blanks at the glare. Not in remorse
—The good not done, the love not given, time
Torn off unused—nor wretchedly because
An only life can take so long to climb
Clear of its wrong beginnings, and may never;
But at the total emptiness for ever,
The sure extinction that we travel to
And shall be lost in always. Not to be here,

Not to be anywhere,
And soon; nothing more terrible, nothing more true.

This is a special way of being afraid
No trick dispels. Religion used to try,
That vast moth-eaten musical brocade
Created to pretend we never die,
And specious stuff that says No rational being
Can fear a thing it will not feel, *not seeing*
That this is what we fear—no sight, no sound,
No touch or taste or smell, nothing to think with,
Nothing to love or link with,
The anaesthetic from which none come round.

And so it stays just on the edge of vision,
A small unfocused blur, a standing chill
That slows each impulse down to indecision.
Most things may never happen: this one will,
And realisation of it rages out
In furnace-fear when we are caught without
People or drink. Courage is no good:
It means not scaring others. Being brave
Lets no one off the grave.
Death is no different whined at than withstood.

Slowly light strengthens, and the room takes shape.
It stands plain as a wardrobe, what we know,
Have always known, know that we can't escape,
Yet can't accept. One side will have to go.

Meanwhile telephones crouch, getting ready to ring
In locked-up offices, and all the uncaring
Intricate rented world begins to rouse.
The sky is white as clay, with no sun.
Work has to be done.
Postmen like doctors go from house to house.

I'm guessing there are at least a few readers out there who have never read this Larkin poem before, and I'm guessing they just got some serious ice in their spines. I've read "Aubade" for thirty years, and it still gives me ice in my spine. I would be worried if it didn't. I once heard a preacher say of this poem, with a breath of relief, that this is *exactly* how he would feel if he weren't a Christian, which seems to me exactly wrong. I don't think it's possible for believers to stand outside of the most powerful achievements of secular art and say "if only that artist could see what we can see," as if their visions were greater than what the artist achieved in the work of art. No, if we have seen properly, then the identification has been too deep: we have participated in the revelation, however dark it has been. That's not to say that some art *isn't* harmful or even demonic. Kafka's concern about the provenance of his inspiration was unnecessary in his case, I think, but not absurd. There aren't many of them, but there do exist a handful of works that, however great (hello, *Lolita*), I wish I had never put in my brain.

"Aubade" is not one of them. One of art's functions is to give form to feelings that would otherwise remain inchoate and corrosive, to give us a means whereby we can inhabit our fears and pains rather than they us, to help us live with our losses rather than being permanently and helplessly haunted by them. I now teach at a divinity school, where many of my students are preparing for the ministry, and they all get a strong shot of Larkin because, as Rowan Williams says, "Preaching is cheap if it fails to meet human beings at their darkest points." It just so happens that Williams is referring to a poet with that sentence: T. S. Eliot.

And here's another thing about "Aubade": it turns out to be, like all great art, a complicated experience. An aubade is a traditional hymn of praise to the morning. One could read that with pure irony, sure, but the poem is devoid of irony. It's damned serious, in fact, and it's hard for me to imagine Larkin resorting to such a crude contrast. Then there's that last line: "Postmen like doctors go from house to house." Doctors come to treat the sick, true, but presumably they also bring healing. Most of all, though, what really complicates the theme of this poem is its form. If you're in *complete* despair, I don't think you find yourself writing a poem, especially not a Bach-like marvel of music and counterpointed language like this one. Gottfried Benn once declared his aspiration to write "the absolute poem, the poem without faith. The poem without hope, the poem addressed to no one, the poem made of words which you assemble in a fascinating way." One could raise the question of whether it's possible to write such a poem, whether the act of creation is itself an act of faith (debatable, as I have suggested). But in any event Benn's departure point is hardly an expression of complete despair. It might even be seen as the opposite.

Jürgen Moltmann once wrote that all honest theology had to be conducted "within earshot of the dying Christ." This poem is in that range—and it *is* theology. Hope is not hope until all ground for hope is lost, to paraphrase Marianne Moore. I feel chilled to the bone by this poem, yet weirdly liberated by its stark, uncompromising clarity. Resurrection is a fiction and a distraction to anyone who refuses to face the reality of death. But to really see this despair clearly—"it stands plain as a wardrobe"—is the first step to being out of it.

Not that it worked out that way for Larkin. "Aubade" was the end of the line for him, and he withered into solitary alcoholic misery. It's not clear why this had to be so, or that it was inevitable. "Aubade" is by no means entirely representative of Larkin's work. He was famous for his sourness, yes, but in fact revelation and resistance were excruciatingly calibrated in him: he was a mystic in a bureaucrat's body, one of the greatest lyric poets in the language who also happened to be a nine-to-five librarian.

Charlie concluded that Larkin's doom lay in his inability to see poetry as a "personally redemptive activity," which is the phrase that really set me off. I think it's dangerous to think of art—or anything, actually—as a *personally* redemptive activity, at least in any ultimate sense. For one thing, it leads to overproduction: if it's art that's saving you, you damn sure better keep producing it, even if the well seems to have run dry. But that's almost beside the point. The real issue, for anyone who suffers the silences of God and seeks real redemption, is that art is not enough. Those spots of time are not enough to hang a life on. At some point you need a *universally* redemptive activity.

You need grace that has nothing to do with your own efforts, for at some point—whether because of disease or despair, exhaustion or loss—you will have no efforts left to make.

And that's just about where I was when I had my exchange with Charlie. I didn't think I was dying, but some part of me—it is difficult to admit this—was ready to. Or no, that's not right. It was more as if I had begun to embrace a truth—*the* truth, actually, the truth to end all truths—that I was meant to resist. Was it the oxycodone and fentanyl, which I was taking in such quantities it's a wonder I didn't simply fail to wake up one morning? Was it exhaustion? Preparing for, undergoing, and then recovering from the bone marrow transplant had taken up an entire year. I ghosted my own clothes—and no doubt the air I shared with others. But no, that's not it either. The thing I felt slipping from me was faith—and slipping from me not like a proposition to which I could no longer assent, but like a life force, the very engine and aim of being. I knew that quote from Rabbi Heschel. I knew this doozy from Geoffrey Hill:

> It is therefore conceivable that a man could refuse to accept the evident signs of grace in his own work; that he himself could never move beyond that "sorrow not mingled with the love of God" [Jeremy Taylor] even though his own poems might speak to others with the voice of hope and love.

I was crammed full of quotes about art and faith and every permutation in between, all of which were subsumed within the one that leapt out at me from Larkin's last poem: "Death is no different whined at than withstood."

I lashed out at Charlie. At least it felt like that to me. I objected to the notion of poetry being a redemptive activity in any ultimate sense, and I objected to his characterization of Larkin as a braver and more stringent writer than George Herbert because Larkin had no overarching metaphysical system with which to bolster his despair and he refused to fabricate one. I don't have the e-mails. I'm pretty sure that if I did have them, they would not reflect the dramatic intensity I am projecting upon them, though it is true to what I felt.

I was so irritable and anxious from the exchange that I had to top off my pain meds with sleeping pills that evening, but I woke at midnight anyway with a fire in my head. I didn't actually recognize the feeling at first, partly because it had been a long time since I had written a real poem, and partly because in those days I woke up with a lot of uninspired fires tearing through me. But then I had the sound and strong governing rhythm of the first two lines—the *sound*, which in poetry does not so much precede as presume sense, have *faith* in it—and by morning the poem was done. As was I. Danielle found me sitting immobile in the living room at dawn, by no means at peace. Nothing had changed. Nothing had . . . *changed*.

It has been my own experience that the reason why there are no atheists in foxholes, so to speak, is not because of the roar of death and destruction that makes a person terrified, but because when one is truly confronted with one's own end, everything goes icily quiet. (James Kugel writes well about this.) You don't turn to God in a crisis because you are afraid, at least not primarily. You turn to God because, for once, all that background chatter in your brain, all that pandemonium of blab, ceases, and you can *hear*—and what some of us hear in those instances is a still, small voice.

I have never felt much comfort in the notion of heaven or eternity, mostly because I can't conceive of these things. But even more than that, Christianity entails—or at least it ought to—a scouring of the self, the individual ego, and as I said above, most of our notions of eternity and/or heaven amount to nothing more than a dream of the self's survival. This is what critics of faith such as Larkin have said for years—that religion is simply a refusal to face our deaths—and they have a strong point.

And yet, and yet . . . there may be some pride at work in that austerity as well, some final refusal of any "psychic peace," as Charlie calls it in "Repression," which is to say: a refusal to be faithful to our moments of faith. Oblivion is one truth. It is devouring us and everything we love. Heaven is the same truth, seen by the light of timelessness that our spots of time, however fugitive or rare, have opened. A poem can be such an opening. "Aubade" expresses an absolute annihilating despair even as it conjures, and implicitly contemplates—and even (I would argue) momentarily submits to—an absolute restorative order.

I don't mean to sound mystical, except inasmuch as there is a persistent, insistent mystery at the center of our existence, which art both derives from and sustains. This mystery is not, in any ultimate sense, explicable to anyone, but it is available to everyone who will not actively resist those moments when the self and all it suffers are finished—again, in both senses of the term. It may happen in art, your own or that of others. It may happen in love, grand or minor. It may happen at any moment in life when, "with an eye made quiet by the power / Of harmony, and the deep power of joy" (Wordsworth), we cease to be ourselves and become, paradoxically, more ourselves. Our souls.

Here, then, is one of my moments of soul. It is set on the Chicago El, which I rode every day to and from the office, packed in with my fellow commuters, whose repressed rage and frustrations I was either exquisitely sensitive to or pathetically projecting (probably some combination of both). "Grand" is the stop in downtown Chicago near where the *Poetry* offices were before we built our new building. "Clark and Division" is another stop earlier on the route. I will always think of this poem as a response to the Larkin poem, and of course to Charlie, to whom I sent it immediately with a gratitude of which it was the only possible expression. "Is it a masterpiece?" as Archibald MacLeish (three Pulitzer Prizes, poet laureate of the United States, and melting, melting . . .) once asked of a snowflake. "Will it last" forever? Certainly not, but forever—for that one night, for this one writer—was in it.

MY STOP IS GRAND

I have no illusion
some fusion
    of force and form

will save me,
bewilderment
        of bonelight
ungrave me

as when the El
shooting through a hell
        of ratty alleys
where nothing thrives
but soot
        and the ratlike lives
that have learned to eat it

screechingly peacocked
a grace of sparks
        so far out and above
the fast curve that jostled
and fastened us
        into a single shock of—
I will not call it love

but at least some brief
and no doubt illusionary belief
        that in one surge of brain
we were all seeing
one thing:
        a lone unearned loveliness
struck from an iron pain.

Already it was gone.
Already it was bone,
    the gray sky
and the encroaching skyline
pecked so clean
    by raptor night
I shuddered at the cold gleam

we hurtled toward
like some insentient herd
    plunging underground at Clark
and Division.
And yet all that day
    I had a kind of vision
that's never gone completely away

of immense clear-paned towers
and endlessly expendable hours
    through which I walked
teeming human streets,
filled with a shine
    that was most intimately me
and not mine.

There are poets for whom death is implicit in every poem they write. Their own deaths, I mean, and not simply the common human condition of mortality, which would be a much-larger category (encompassing every work of art ever made, perhaps). It is as if an unresolved existential crisis ignited every inspiration, no matter how vital, and soldered shut every finished form.

Larkin is like this. Even his epiphanies, for all their head-freshening clarity (and reality-stabilizing security), come trailing clouds of elegy. If he's going to write about a room, you can bet it's a room that's been abandoned ("Home Is So Sad"). Behind the "sun-comprehending glass" of "High Windows"—a revelatory image that rips open that poem in the way a poem can rip open a life—is a blue oblivion that is "nothing, and is nowhere, and is endless." These poems sound universal, but aren't really. The generality is a disguise for a fear that is raw, specific, and, until "Aubade," mostly deflected.

The same dynamic (minus the indirection) is evident in the poems of Sylvia Plath, though her obvious mental illness makes the phrase *unresolved existential crisis* seem inadequate, and her suicide might seem to make my observation self-evident. But biographical details are beside the point here. Plath could be alive and writing wry dispatches from her rest home in Wellesley, and the same implacable yet weirdly personal energy of unbeing would freeze the first-time reader of *Ariel*.

Then there are those poets in whose work you feel not their deaths, but their lives, not aversion, but appetite. They are not at all the "opposite" of the former group, but in fact vivid kin. They too have an unresolved existential crisis (maybe the same one?) churning in them, but it heightens rather than inflames sensation, drives their minds into the earth rather than out of it.

Hart Crane is a prime example and, because like Plath he committed suicide at a young age, further evidence that the energy I am trying to isolate in the poems is not contingent on what happens in the life. But Crane's fate—he was alcoholic and hurled himself into the sea at age thirty-two—does suggest that there are dangers for this temperament as well. The critic Yvor Winters, who was a friend of Crane's, wrote after his death that subsequent poets ought to read him in mostly a monitory way, so that they might recognize and avoid "a new mode of damnation." I once wrote an essay with that very title in which I agreed with Winters's analysis but disagreed with his conclusion, which assumed that all poets have a *choice* about the way that art and life, ambition and survival, play out in them. Twenty years later, many losses lighter, I'm not so sure.

I still believe in the visionary reach—and the very real risk—of certain kinds of art. I still believe there can be callings in which deliverance and destruction are raveled up in ways that, to an outside observer, might seem like madness.

("Whoever would save his life will lose it . . .") Perhaps there is even some sense in which, for the genuine artist, there is no such thing as a *resolved* existential crisis. (Consider the examples: late Tolstoy, late Wordsworth, most of Winters, actually—zombies all.) I do feel, though, that there is some viable middle course between vision and will, some way of productively harnessing rather than either suffering or enslaving one's spiritual turmoil. In fact, I know there is, because I have seen it.

THE LAST TIME I SAW Craig Arnold, he was headed on a trip around the world to complete a book—part prose and part poetry—about volcanoes. I remember thinking at the time that it was as if he'd found physical expression for the spiritual fire that burned so ardently in him. I don't like to think that thought anymore.

I first met Craig twenty years ago at Lynchburg College in Virginia, where he was part of a symposium of young poets I had organized. Tall, lean, and with his head shaved, clad in black leather pants and a tight white T-shirt, he didn't "read" his poems: he performed them, strutting elastically about as if he were onstage, whipsawing lines and limbs in precise, rehearsed ways, electrifying that quaint little lecture hall as if it were the Moulin Rouge. I tend to be allergic to this kind of self-dramatization in poetry, but I loved it. All of it: the flair that seemed to arise naturally out of his character rather than being appliquéd on; the mercurial and protean nature of his subjects (and, I would learn, his own life); the hell-bent hungers and raptures kept in check—or at least kept intact, intelligible—by the tough-minded conscience and craft that ran through the poems like a spine.

Those were the poems of *Shells*, Craig's first book, which had been selected by W. S. Merwin for the Yale Series of Younger Poets in 1998, the same year my own first book came out with a press that is now, and practically was then, defunct. I felt the distinction keenly and recall with nauseating lucidity the dinner at which, to all three of the poets present, I declared the event to be, for all of us, a competition. It was meant to be a joke, but no doubt the acid in me trickled into the tone just a bit. It made for an awkward moment, which Craig quickly rescued. "No one could compete with you, Chris," he said with a smile that managed to be understanding, companionable, and just a tad reproachful all at once.

Nine years would pass between the publication of *Shells* and the appearance of Craig's next book, *Made Flesh*, nine years in which Craig lived in Rome and Bogotá and Wyoming and Utah and I don't know where else. It was in some ways the typical twenty-first-century up-and-coming American poet's life—the pickup jobs and the scramble for publishers, the rescuing fellowships and provisional relationships (for the last six years of his life, though, Craig was very happily partnered with another poet, Rebecca Lindenberg), the constant effort to find a way of staying alive without allowing one's lifeblood to congeal into a career.

And yet it wasn't so typical: Craig was perhaps the only poet I have known personally—the only good poet, I should say—who seemed completely at ease with being a poet. Don't get me wrong: he had all the existential friction and psychic disquiet we've come to expect from post-Romantic poets. (Crane was a formative influence.) You don't have to read his poems autobiographically—and they're too cunningly, winningly imagined to do that—to get a hint of the tempest that was their source. But he also had, right down to his soul (I guess it *was* his soul), a calm and clarifying equanimity about his purpose on this earth, and always over the years, when I would encounter him, I would discover my own bristling insecurities melting away in his presence and feel my own relationship with poetry renewed. This wasn't because he had achieved some sort of monkish calm with regard to ambition, and it certainly wasn't because he was placidly and brainlessly open to everything he encountered (in fact, he could be quite sudden and sharp in his opinions). No, what Craig had, besides his endless and endlessly inclusive charisma, was a capacity to be at once completely grounded in the physical world and in his own body and yet mysteriously permeable. I'm not sure how this played out in his daily life, but I know it affected mine, and for the better. I also know that this quality gives the concrete things of his poetry, and especially his later poetry, a powerful sense of being more themselves by being more *than* themselves.

MEDITATION ON A GRAPEFRUIT

To wake when all is possible
before the agitations of the day

have gripped you
             To come to the kitchen
and peel a little basketball
for breakfast
          To tear the husk
like cotton padding   a cloud of oil
misting out of its pinprick pores
clean and sharp as pepper
                    To ease
each pale pink section out of its case
so carefully   without breaking
a single pearly cell
             To slide each piece
into a cold blue china bowl
the juice pooling   until the whole
fruit is divided from its skin
and only then to eat
          so sweet
                a discipline
precisely pointless   a devout
involvement of the hands and senses
a pause   a little emptiness

each year harder to live within
each year harder to live without

There is so much that I love about this poem, not least how the ravenous passions of Craig's first book ("Hot," a long poem about a "love" for psychotically hot chili peppers, is the centerpiece) have been transformed into a hunger that is so much more deliberate, attentive, and sustaining. But also there are the sly rhymes, the clarity and briskness of detail ("sharp as pepper"!), the humor (that "little basketball"). Or consider the space-ghosted form of the lines, so apt for their subject, and the way that space in the last two lines of the poem is suddenly gone—just as any spot of time, as it vanishes back into the life it had so fully illuminated, is gone. I love how the poem contains in miniature the sense of accelerating time that age intensifies—the "agitations of the day" at the beginning have become, by the end, entire years—and how that moment is salvaged as a resource for future rescue and renewal. And I love—maybe this most of all—that the poem really is about, in the end, eating a grapefruit. They need not be Damascus raptures, our moments of soul.

I first read this poem on the morning of April 27, 2009, and immediately e-mailed an elated acceptance to Craig. It was a surprise when I didn't hear from him that first day. Poetry can be a lonely business, and Craig was no different from most poets in that he tended to respond with great alacrity to acceptances. Another day passed, and I assumed he was simply without Internet access. His research took him to some extremely isolated parts of the planet. And then, on the twenty-ninth, reports began to trickle in about a poet gone missing on a remote Japanese island on the evening of April 27, and it wasn't long before I realized that at roughly the very time I was writing Craig to praise him for a poem that had restored me to the earth, he was vanishing off its face forever. For that's what happened. Despite a massive international effort, nothing of Craig was ever found, aside from some tracks leading up to an abyss—into which, it is assumed by everyone, he fell. There is no reason to think otherwise. Craig was happy and healthy, as anyone who had seen him before he died could attest.

Me, for instance. I had seen Craig just a few weeks earlier, when he came into town for the huge annual writers conference that was held in Chicago that year. He showed up at the *Poetry* offices one afternoon and practically lifted me off the floor in a hug. As always, the twitchy intelligence, the solar flares of his energy, surprised me—and, as always, surprised a happiness in me I hadn't known was there. We locked him in an office all afternoon in hopes that he would write the long-overdue prose note to the translation he had done for an upcoming issue, and for hours he sat there (weird: how suddenly still he could become, how creaturely focused), finally emerging near dusk with a single brilliant and self-revealing page on a poet he had recently met while living in Colombia ("to hit upon such an image requires an intimate acquaintance with all the flavors of pain and persistence and hopelessness—here, I thought, was a conscience to reckon with"). The next day, Craig led—with great generosity, and much to my surprise—a reading he'd shaped as a celebration of the magazine. He'd given up the extravagant reading style of years before because, he said, he began to think it was actually deflecting people's attention and detracting from the work. Still, even understated (as if that word could ever be used for Craig!), he was searing, mesmerizing, unforgettable.

Craig stayed with Danielle and me that week, and somehow, in between the dozens of friends he was seeing, or tending to, or shuttling to and from the airport, we found time to talk. I remember most clearly his last morning in our little house in North Chicago, when he made us *migas* for breakfast, and the conversation turned to something he and I had talked of many times over the years: the necessary but destabilizing intensities of poetry, and the life that one risks by cultivating those intensities, and the life that—in some cases, our cases, we both felt—poetry also rescues. Out in the front yard, he gave me another of his no-holds-barred hugs and promised to be back in August. Only as he drove off did I realize I'd forgotten to get him to sign our copy of *Made Flesh*, which is a shame, since the inscription he wrote for me on *Shells* all those years ago is a gem. Filling the entire page, and linking quotations from *Fight Club* and Baudelaire with a self-consciously absurd smiley face, it's Craig all over. "I hope this stays with you," he scrawled on the very last bit of space at the end of the page. "I certainly will."

t occurs to me—for the first time—that I have no idea what Craig believed. What "faith" he had, I mean. I put the word in quotes not to ironize its meaning, but to widen it; though he may have had no faith any religion would recognize, Craig certainly had one that I did. But after all my encounters with him, both in person and on the page, and though I attended a moving memorial service in which one person after another stood up and gave testament to the effect his presence had on their lives, I still have no idea whether Craig saw himself as a religious person or not.

And can't quite bring myself to care. How stale our spiritual language can sometimes seem in the face of a rare, clear spirit. I don't really believe in atheists. Nor in true believers, for that matter. One either lives toward God or not. The word *God* is of course an abyss, bright or dark depending on the day. But there is no middle ground, no cautious agnosticism in which to settle, no spiritual indifference that is not, even when accompanied by high refinement and exquisite intelligence, torpor. I know the necessity of religion. I know we need communal ritual and meaningful creeds. And yet I know, too, that all of this emerges from an intuition so original that, in some ultimate sense, to define is to defile. One either lives toward God or not.

But how do I reconcile all this with my resistance to C. K. Williams's notion of poetry being a personally redemptive activity? Or my feeling that Karl Barth, a theologian whose scriptural insistences often baffle and irritate me, is nevertheless onto something with that line he draws between human and divine inspiration? How does one acknowledge the eclectic and syncretic spiritual impulses of modern culture, a culture of which I am a grateful and indebted participant, without betraying the grace that has at times not simply given that culture a coherent aim—all of Christianity, for all its obvious faults, is this—but also lifted my own life out of despair. I hear people complain about the loss of any sense of the sacred in contemporary culture, but, as the Polish philosopher Leszek Kołakowski has underlined, the real danger (and loss) lies not in the fact that secular culture denies sacred experience, but that we discover it everywhere. Half a century ago Karl Barth recognized and even partially ratified this tendency in what is probably his most famous saying: "God may speak to us through Russian Communism, through a flute concerto, through a blossoming shrub or through a dead dog. We shall do well to listen to him if he really does so." But Barth also recognized that if everything is sacred, then nothing is. Thus this clear but not exactly clarifying proviso: "The Gospel is not a truth among other truths. Rather, it sets a question mark against all truths."

I ONCE SPENT a miserable winter in a magnificent house in Paris. Never are we more susceptible to the vagaries of fate than when we have convinced ourselves that there is such a thing. Fate, I mean. An explicit and exotic destination at a time when I was nearly overcome with aimlessness, a rent-free house right next to the Luxembourg Gardens, four glorious months in which to finally find my way to the poems that had been eluding me: What could go wrong?

Rats, for one thing, which seethed in the walls of my bedroom like something out of Céline. French, next, which simply would not condescend to exist on my Texas tongue and thus sealed me in a cone of loneliness and despair like . . . something out of Céline. And finally, futilely, there was poetry, which proved to be even more elusive than French.

Months passed. Or didn't pass so much as congeal around me. It took all my energy to walk to the corner *boulangerie* for a baguette.

It has been my experience that faith, like art, is most available when I cease to seek it, cease even to believe in it, perhaps, if by belief one means that busy attentiveness, that purposeful modern consciousness that *knows* its object. One morning, instead of sitting down to rage at a blank page, I grabbed a copy of *Don Quixote* (Walter Starkie translation) from the bookshelves. I looked up three days later, and the ice of time had cracked.

Just like that, the poems began to come, or rather, the poem began to come, because it was quickly evident that every piece was part of some emerging whole. It was the tone of *Quixote* that freed me, as if some existential key had been slipped into the lock of my soul. People tend to think of *Quixote* as a comic novel, and it certainly is that, but underneath its ironic and sardonic surface, which is to say underneath the mad and antic character of Quixote himself, there is a current that is quiet, constant, and heartbreakingly sane. Madness is something he seems to both suffer and wield—which is to say that there is a tragedy awaiting him, as there is anyone whose reality is disfigured by a despair that can be, for a time, transformed (what is Quixote but the consummate modern artist?) but never fully dispelled.

For a month, I hardly slept, hardly left the house. I muffled the creative mania with ever-increasing amounts of alcohol each evening, but by three or four I was up pacing and raving again. The onslaught ended with a comic confrontation with God. Literally: the character I had invented—the character who was so roughly reinventing me—finally demands that God make an appearance and account for himself. God declines, or seems to. And yet, though I was still a few years from making a conscious return to any kind of formal faith, I can see now that it was while reading *Don Quixote* that wretched winter in Paris in that rat-walled redoubt of loneliness and silence that the real movement in my heart began. "And some say he smiled like a man forgiven" is a line from the last page of that long poem. And I did. And I was.

AND NOTHING CHANGED. I left Paris and went back to San Francisco and the relationship that had no futurity to it and thus exerted its death even in—perhaps especially in—our moments of life and happiness. I went back to the work, whose ultimate aim I still would not acknowledge, and thus suffered like an unconscious trauma what should have been conscious joy. I edited *Poetry* and fell in love and got sick and, when I could no longer lift a hand to help myself, Being itself seemed to reach one down to me. And nothing . . . *changed.*

I MET SEAMUS HEANEY in person only once, at a dinner in Chicago after a reading he did for *Poetry* during my last year at the magazine. A few months later he would be dead. Meeting him was a momentous event for me, though in a way it was impossible for me to meet the man, for I knew so much of his work not simply by heart, but by bone and nerve. The poems had become authorless inside of me, so unmediated that I flinched whenever he got the cadence "wrong" in one of my particular favorites, such as the famous elegy to his aunt, "Sunlight":

There was a sunlit absence.
The helmeted pump in the yard
heated its iron,
water honeyed

in the slung bucket
and the sun stood
like a griddle cooling
against the wall

of each long afternoon.
So, her hands scuffled
over the bakeboard,
the reddening stove

sent its plaque of heat
against her where she stood
in a floury apron
by the window.

Now she dusts the board
with a goose's wing,
now sits, broad-lapped,
with whitened nails

and measling shins:
here is a space
again, the scone rising
to the tick of two clocks.

And here is love
like a tinsmith's scoop
sunk past its gleam
in the meal-bin.

It turned out that Heaney was reading *me*: galleys of a prose book I was about to publish on faith, death, pain, poetry. (We shared an editor.) My stunned silence left plenty of space for a compliment, which he smilingly declined to pay. I rather appreciated that, though at the time I couldn't say why.

Later, in the middle of dinner, and in the middle of a conversation that had nothing whatsoever to do with religious faith, he leaned over to me and said—very quietly, he seemed frail to me—that he felt caught between the old forms of faith that he had grown up with in Northern Ireland and some new dispensation that had not yet emerged. That was trying to emerge. I had spent much of the past few years talking about this subject to audiences of one sort or another. That very morning, in fact, I had flown back to Chicago from New Haven and my final interview at Yale Divinity School, where I had already decided to begin teaching courses on . . . art and faith. You'd think I would have had something ready to hand, something about art being one of the chief ways in which faith is being remade for our age, something about religion having lost its claims on the definition of faith, something about the eerie ways in which the work of a half-believer, an agnostic— hell, even an atheist who is genuinely intent on *disclosing reality* ("Aubade"!)—can be the tool that clears the ground for the ground of being.

But no. Silence. Again, though it confused and disturbed me at the time, I'm glad for this glitch in the predictable.

I do feel that there's truth in these statements about art and faith—and Heaney's work seems to me a moving example—but just as there are truths we can see only at a slant, there are truths the very authenticity of which depends upon their not being uttered. The "meaning" of suffering is often like this. (And isn't this mostly what that Heaney poem above is "about"?) And so is the meaning of great poetry, much of which derives from some version of that very premise— "Glimmerings are what the soul's composed of," as Heaney has it—and much of which exists in order to protect and preserve just such glimmerings:

Now she dusts the board
with a goose's wing,
now sits, broad-lapped,
with whitened nails

and measling shins:
here is a space
again, the scone rising
to the tick of two clocks.

There are poets who take you to the edge of language, either with words that begin to ease out of their referents (Mallarmé, Mandelstam, Hopkins, Eliot, Crane, Stevens) or with abstractions handled so concretely that you are jolted into an uncanny receptiveness anterior to "belief" or "disbelief" (Dickinson, Wilbur, Eliot again, Stevens again, Anne Carson). This is not a kind of zombie mellifluousness in the first instance, and it's not a baffling complexity in the second. It is a capacity within language to match—or, really, to *be*—the unity that is at the heart of matter. Unity and clarity are not necessarily coextensive. There can be a kind of clarity that is bewilderment, and there can be a kind of bewilderment that reorients one's spirit.

Heaney's particular gifts lay elsewhere. It's not simply that he either lacked or distrusted the capacity for making poetry pass over into pure music, and thus hewed to the discrete, almost plodding, eye-to-the-ground notations one hears even in a poem as musically refined as "Sunlight"; and it's not that, even unbelieving, he avoided giving expression to the numinous. He sought to "credit marvels," as he put it, and much of his later work is a deliberate attempt to render just such intuitions and insights. That it is so conspicuously *deliberate* is sometimes the problem.

No, what Heaney could do is take that inchoate edge of existence and give it actual edges. He could bring the cosmic into the commonplace. (Very different, mind you, from that cliché of discovering the extraordinary in the ordinary.) He could make matter, inside the space of a poem, immortal, or make the concept of eternity, in more than one sense, matter.

Take that word *love*, for instance, in the poem above. Now there's a word the gleam's gone out of. There's one of those edge-of-experience abstractions of which Ezra Pound taught us to "go in fear." And rightly so, too, because it often enters a poem the way *God* enters a poem, apologetically almost, or, worse, automatically, in any event with an air of failure to it, a big sign posted next to a big abyss that says This Way to All That I Cannot Say.

It may be true, as Mallarmé thought, that poetry's duty is "to purify the language of the tribe," but I think we have tended to hear in that statement an injunction of radical innovation rather than recovery, of creation rather than resuscitation. I am most moved in Heaney's poems by these moments when physical things acquire an uncanny porousness, as if human life, and more than human life, were suddenly streaming through them; and when metaphysical concepts—love, for instance—can suddenly seem almost tangible, at once authentically time-bound and defiantly timeless.

And here is love
like a tinsmith's scoop
sunk past its gleam
in the meal-bin.

Outside the restaurant, Heaney and I embraced and both hoped our paths would cross again. It seemed likely, as I had never been to Ireland and was suddenly determined to go. And then, as he prepared to get in the cab with his wife, he did an odd thing. He turned around and caught my eye, then winked. There was something self-consciously paternal and literary about the gesture, edged with irony and affection both, the action of a man who had long since grown accustomed to the fact that his actions would be memorialized in the minds of others. I thought immediately and inevitably of his elegy to Robert Lowell, which ends with the two men parting and Lowell whispering—"risking," as Heaney puts it—"'I'll pray for you.'"

There is one more thing. That evening with Heaney had, for me, an element of grace to it. I had flown home from New Haven that very morning with my life—and the way I had always thought about the role of poetry in my life—on the verge of a great change. ("Everything in you must bow down," a student told me his bishop had told him that very morning, words that suddenly iced my own spine just as completely as "Aubade.") But also, during Heaney's reading, it was as if each poem conjured up the self I was when I had first read it. Then the intimate conversation at dinner, the revelations each of us made and did not make, that meaningful wink! It all seemed a great gift to me, and no small part of that gift was its formally coherent quality, as if life were, for once, art. So it was quite a surprise, and not a pleasant one, when I walked into the offices of the Poetry Foundation the next morning and saw Heaney again.

I'd been up half the night, partly with excitement and partly with the old anxieties that the excitement stoked. Was I doing the right thing in leaving *Poetry* and moving to a divinity school? Did I even have sufficient faith in God to justify talking about that to people preparing to stake their lives on him? And what would this mean for my poetry? Or is the question "What does an authentic life in poetry look like?" the same as asking "What does an authentic faith look like?" As I suggested, I'm pretty sure that even the old alcoholic and imploding atheist Philip Larkin was, with "Aubade," rousing himself to answer a call to which that poem was not simply an adequate answer but the only one possible, just as I'm sure that the poet had faith in something that the man, afterward, could not. Not Christianity, for Christ's sake, but *something*. In fact, I suspect that what he felt, for the brief time he was so beautifully singing his despair, was what every artist feels when mind and matter seem to be open to each other, seem, even, to see into each other: joy.

And then it was done. As was Larkin, who could never muster faith even in Heschel's sense, could never believe in the order that his own poems had opened to him. Heaney, as his comment to me reveals, was not entirely different. Though he actively attended and nourished what he called "the marvelous," and though he was clearly a man of great balance and sanity, with an enviable web of warm relationships, his unprompted comment to me suggests that he still felt some rift between the revelations of his art and the reality of his life. I have no idea if this rift caused him pain. I wouldn't have thought so, had he not made his comment to me at dinner and left such a conspicuous space for me to fill. What might I have said? *All you have to do, Seamus, is open your big Irish heart to Jesus.* One more truth that dies with the utterance. No, the casual way that American Christians have of talking about God is not simply dispiriting, but is, for some sensibilities, actively destructive. There are times when silence is not only the highest, but the only possible, piety. I'd like to think that he and I, in our respective ways, were acknowledging that fact.

He stood with his wife and a couple of foundation employees about fifty feet from me. His back was turned. I knew that small talk was the only talk possible, and that it was, for me, impossible. Hurriedly, a little shamefully, I slipped into my office before anyone could see me (I hope!) and closed the door.

I ran my motor fast much of my life seeking the saving absolute. There is no such item to be found. I
had known these thoughts for a long time, and they
meant very little, until I *experienced* them. I remember
the hour I experienced them. Nothing changed, and
yet everything changed. Grief, fear, love, life, death,
everything goes on just as before, but now everything
seems lifted, just a bit, into its own being.

That's Ammons from a late letter to Harold Bloom.
Ammons doesn't directly link this mystical experience
with the one he had mentioned to Josephine Miles two decades
earlier, but it seems obvious that he is still obsessed with—and
faithful to?—whatever mysterious revelation happened to him
at some point in the past. And though he makes no mention
of Maritain this time around, the ghost of those ideas still hov-
ers near. Early in *Creative Intuition in Art and Poetry*, in a passage about Paul Cézanne, Maritain writes about the power of
art to convey "the architectural authority with which Things
exist and, at the same time, the austere serenity with which
they confront our dreams." (I think of Wordsworth and the
moment in *The Prelude* when the offended mountains pur-
sue the young poet and are a "trouble to [his] dreams.") Both

Ammons and Maritain, in their respective ways, posit a hard material truth that is expansive and enlivening rather than, like Larkin's, constrictive and dispiriting. To say that there is no saving absolute is not to say that there is nothing that saves.

Ammons felt that the failure of the absolute freed him to feel the truth of contingent matter, which is the only truth. This is not a Death-is-the-mother-of-beauty discovery à la early Stevens. It is more a discovery that being has no antecedent. But this, in turn, is by no means the end of God. All of Ammons's best poems—for me, his entire life's work distills down to eight or nine permanent epiphanies—reveal this. His insistence on things as they are includes some metaphysical lift and slippage that is also true to things as they are, some flicker of spirit among the adamant facts.

But what does one *do* with that knowledge, which is not really knowledge, even typed out in sentences as I have just done, but a kind of physical experience, an intuition in the blood? "The City Limits," the poem with which I began this book, ends with a recognition that "the dark / work of the deepest cells is of a tune with May bushes," a line I never heard implying cancer until I had it, but now can't unhear, thank God, since the poem's final realization/revelation describes a transformation of one's entire relation to reality: "and fear lit by the breadth of such calmly turns to praise." This revelation happens in a poem, true, but a poem is part of a life, even the ones you only read. Maybe especially those, actually, since to finish a work of art is to be exiled from it. But perhaps if one lives long enough, and fails fruitfully enough, then the existential tension between all the old antinomies—imagination and experience, art and life, God and Not—might, at moments, be eased.

THE PLANET ON THE TABLE

Ariel was glad he had written his poems.
They were of a remembered time
Or of something seen that he liked.

Other makings of the sun
Were waste and welter
And the ripe shrub writhed.

His self and the sun were one
And his poems, although makings of his self,
Were no less makings of the sun.

It was not important that they survive.
What mattered was that they should bear
Some lineament or character,

Some affluence, if only half-perceived,
In the poverty of their words,
Of the planet of which they were part.

That's Wallace Stevens. *Late* Wallace Stevens, I should add—a resigned, resilient, skeletal little poem I must have read right past in my preparations for that debacle conference in Connecticut all those years ago. Now I know of no better—which is to say no truer, which is to say it is permanently ungraspable and thus permanently available—statement of the spiritual reward in writing. But not just in writing. "And his poems, although makings of his self, / Were no less makings of the sun." This is just what Ammons aimed at with his impersonal "I": to assert and to assent at the same time, to bow down to the original energy to which one also stakes a claim. It is to reside, if only for an instant, in the universal coherence that enables, to adapt Maritain's language, things and dreams to have one being.

When I was young, I wanted only to imprint one poem on eternity, which is to say: to serve the muse I would one day master. In my early forties, in love and near death, I had the image of hanging on a huge hook, like some creature whose resistance only worsened its plight, and it wasn't until writing this book that I recognized the source of the image.

> *He held radical light*
> *as music in his skull: music*
> *turned, as*
> *over ridges immanences of evening light*
> *rise, turned*
> *back over the furrows of his brain*
> *into the dark, shuddered,*
> *shot out again*
> *in long swaying swirls of sound:*
>
> *reality had little weight in his transcendence*
> *so he*

had trouble keeping
his feet on the ground, was
terrified by that
and liked himself, and others, mostly
under roofs:
nevertheless, when the
light churned and changed

his head to music, nothing could keep him
off the mountains, his
head back, mouth working,
wrestling to say, to cut loose
from the high unimaginable hook:
released, hidden from stars, he ate,
burped, said he was like any one
of us: demanded he
was like any one of us.

It's Ammons, a poem I clearly remember first reading early one icy morning of 1988, deep in the stacks of the Washington and Lee library. I slept there sometimes that winter because, though I lived in a mansion that in its day must have been truly glorious, the only room that I could afford—the metaphors come showering down on me now—had no heat.

For a time I would say I was released from this hook by faith, a faith that did not originate in me, but came from elsewhere, or from so deep inside of me that I could not claim it—a faith that, I should add, I cannot recover now. But I would also now say that it was ambition that released me from ambition. "The best way out is always through," said Robert Frost, who himself wriggled on one long, sharp, and never-quite-nameable existential predicament. If I say that the hook is God, will only believers understand me? If I say that the hook is the Void, will only atheists understand me? The hook is both God and Void, grace and pain. I am reasonably sure that most poets will know what I mean.

Certainly Danielle does. For me, the greatest revelation of love has been that revelation can be shared. When theologians say that God is love, they are not stating an equation. "The God who *is* does not exist," as Bonhoeffer said. But neither is the statement simply a metaphor. God is present wherever genuine love is present, or perhaps more accurately, God, who is omnipresent but often experienced as absence, is *made available* through the expression of genuine love. The life of God and the life of humans are—for this one time and in this one way—one thing. This doesn't mean that some form of shared human love is necessary for revelation. God comes to the loveless and the loneliest among us, as the whole histories of art and faith attest. But perhaps love is necessary for revelation to *remain* revelation. That poem I wrote after my exchange with Charlie Williams was a great access of speech and spirit in my own life, the huge stone of despair lifted from my tongue. But in order for that moment to be more than a moment, and for that love to be more than literature, I needed to share it with the woman with whom I share a life. By "it" I do not mean the poem itself, of course, but the faithful and feeling being of the man who wrote it.

I fear I'm sounding wise. "I desire the ease of wisdom,"

said Ammons, "but have been unwilling to surrender the madness of poetry." Me too. And me neither. Nevertheless, I do not hang in the same helpless way from that old hopeless hook. Not as a writer: the door to my study is open, and my daughters' lives mean infinitely more to me than my own work. And not as a reader: I have come to value the stark and merely mortal concessions of Stevens's late work as well as the self-conscious strut and masterpiece atmosphere of the early poems. (The long poems of pure abstraction still seem to me a wasteland.) There is much argument over whether or not Stevens converted to Catholicism on his deathbed. I yawn just pondering it. Not because it doesn't matter, but because the claim of God is too individual, intimate, and inarticulate to admit of this kind of schoolbook speculation. The creative faith evident in "The Planet on the Table" is enough for me, as is the proud bow before oblivion. "They also live," as Archibald MacLeish continues in "The Snowflake," "who swerve and vanish in the river." But I should add that the poem is enough because it enacts and acknowledges its own insufficiency. It is reconciled to some degree of exile from an order that it does not renounce and thereby makes of its own oblivion a kind of lens, rather than mere end. "Lord," wrote Julia Randall, who slipped into that mystic river in 2005 and whose life's work seems sure to follow, "that I am a moment of your turnings."

I left *Poetry* in the summer of 2013 and moved with my family to Hamden, Connecticut, two doors down from a modest brick Tudor-ish home in which, our real estate agent told us in an aside one day, a famous poet had been born and raised. The town had even devoted a day to him the year before, she said, with a big event in City Hall timed to coincide with the poet's birthday. You could find it all memorialized on a plaque outside the library, as indeed my daughters did and still do, running up the walk most weekends to claim and proclaim the name that our real estate agent could not quite bring to mind: *Donald Hall!*

One of the first things we did was drive the three hours up to Eagle Pond Farm in New Hampshire to see him and Linda, whom Don describes in *Essays After Eighty* as "butch with pretty dimples, an Old Woman of the Mountain in bone structure." She is serenely high-spirited, fluent in French and silence, Yankee plain in opinion and action. She works at a shelter for battered women, and her poems are compact charms that don't express meaning so much as defiantly, and somehow buoyantly, deflect it.

We sipped sherry (at Don's insistence, and with a twist of wry) and settled in. The girls were just three then, and they raced around the wildflowered yard and clambered around the attic, playing house with the house that was no playhouse ("Weep for what little things could make them glad"), skipping back down to climb right into Don's abundant beard like wood sprites in a willow tree. He had, in his mid-eighties, exchanged his unfiltered Camels for an e-cigarette, and he rarely left his chair, surrounded by books and papers and smoldering with memories. There was the time he and Geoffrey Hill, both in their early twenties, got into an actual fistfight outside a pub near Oxford because Hill was so upset that Don had decided to return to the United States. There was the conversation he had at a literary festival with Philip Roth, who had to lean down because Don was confined to a wheelchair.

> ROTH: How are you doing?
> DON, with a shrug: Still writing.
> ROTH, with a shrug: What else is there?

And of course there was Jane Kenyon, the graduate student at Michigan Don had loved for seventeen radiant years and then grieved for even longer. For people in the poetry world, this story is perhaps too familiar to pierce anymore, but one day readers may happen upon certain words that grace and pain conspired to create, and may feel a flash of pastness enlivening their very nerves.

SUMMER KITCHEN

In June's high light she stood at the sink
*   With a glass of wine,*
And listened for the bobolink,
And crushed garlic in late sunshine.

I watched her cooking, from my chair.
*   She pressed her lips*
Together, reached for kitchenware,
And tasted sauce from her fingertips.

"It's ready now. Come on," she said.
*   "You light the candle."*
We ate, and talked, and went to bed,
And slept. It was a miracle.

Reputation embalms a person. Before I knew him personally, Don seemed to me the living emblem of the literary establishment, a tall, carved Harvard hunk of whiteness, the everywhere editor and anthologist, friend of Henry Moore and George Plimpton, chronicler of the great modernists, most of whom he had known personally. (If you haven't read *Their Ancient Glittering Eyes*, which is shamefully out of print, you have missed a splendid book.) In fact, civilization—or should I say our particular commodified and overprogrammed version of it, because Don roams at home through the deep past—has little purchase on him, and his mind, even now, is as wild and rampant as the truck-and-plunder in which he lives.

Much has been written about the effort of the lyric poem to stop time, to seize some tiny eternity with the music of a moment. And indeed, *music* is the operative word here. If reality is, as this entire book has been arguing, perceived truly only when the truth of its elusiveness is part of that perception ("I only recognize her going"), and if poetry has any reach into ultimate reality at all, it is the abstract element of music in which that connection is most deeply felt. I am thinking of the ramifying concretion and ungainsayable fluency of poems like "Hymn" and "The City Limits," the deliberate, almost anti-transcendent clarity of "Sunlight" or "Meditation on a Grapefruit." I am thinking, too, of the homemade lines and rhymes of "Summer Kitchen," which reads as if it had been thrown together with any old materials lying around, as indeed it was. And suddenly I recall another observation to place alongside that earlier fragment from the man whose imminent execution made him fear not for his future, but his past. "Nothing is lost," writes Bonhoeffer at the same time, from the same grim cell. "In Christ all things are taken up, preserved, albeit in transfigured form, transparent, clear, liberated from the torment of self-serving demands." This was written, it just so happens, in the margin of a sixteenth-century musical score that Bonhoeffer had transcribed from memory and could hear only—but could hear utterly—in his head. "Magnificent," he wrote as those ghostly notes sounded in and out of time, rooting him in and out of time: "consummately consoling."

But that is a mystical claim for the power of art, not a practical one. It is about bringing eternity into one's immediate consciousness rather than, as so many poets have tried to do, as so many people try to do in one way or another, projecting one's consciousness into eternity. (And of course Bonhoeffer is also talking about the rescuing effect of someone else's art, not his own.) What hope is there to survive "Devouring time," Shakespeare asks over and over again in his sonnets, and over and over he gives a version of this answer: "O, none, unless this miracle have might, / That in black ink my love may still shine bright." Who would even think such a thing now, much less say it? Who would claim such power for art? For that matter, who would claim such power—and really *mean* it, in their bones, as I think Bonhoeffer did—for God?

I'm usually suspicious of claims that privilege one generation's experience, always of some form of suffering, over another's. (Why do we never compare our joys or our relative capacities for experiencing joy?) Contemporary culture is awash with anxiety over the disease of anxiety, the endless onslaught of technology, and the diminishment of individual attention our electronic immersion entails. It's a genuine problem, no question, one I feel myself, but it's not as new or as dependent upon contemporary technology as we make it out to be. Way back in 1790, in his "Preface to *Lyrical Ballads*," Wordsworth decried the "degrading thirst after outrageous stimulation" against which his poetry—interior, meditative, focused on common people and things—was trying to find an audience. The argument is more eloquent and sophisticated than we're used to, but the heart of his critique would make a fine tweet.

Still, some ruptures are real. The battle between individual consciousness and the social reality within which that consciousness acquires and sustains its existence may be recogniz-able, but what does seem different—and attenuated—is the sense of distinctiveness, solidity, and autonomy we attribute to individual consciousness. Wordsworth believed that every person contained within him- or herself memories—"those first affections, / Those shadowy recollections"—that not only bore the impress of some preexisting glory, but suggested a transcendent unity to which we were destined to return. And *therefore*, every individual consciousness, every observed detail in every life, had cosmic value and consequence. This is the only reason that a diminished attention might matter.

Now the world is not only too much with us, as Words-worth said, distracting us from our true selves, but too little with us as well. Or, to put it differently, we are too little within the world that science has both opened up to us and hurled us howling into. The eyes with which you are reading these words are formed from matter and energy that had its origin in an unimaginably massive and mysteriously creative "bang" almost fourteen billion years ago. And while you were reading the previous sentence, something like two hundred miles of space was added to the reality that emerged from that initial instant. Every single second, existence leaps some fifty-three miles farther into . . . what, exactly? Something that was not in any way something. (*Tautology!* I hear my irony-primed, eight-year-old daughters cry out at our dinner table.) It is a strange state of affairs (though one that certain ancient theologians would have recognized) to be able to speak a thing you can't conceive, to be in possession of knowledge that you cannot, in any meaningful sense, know.

Nor is that the only new vertigo, for that same accelerating immensity is mirrored, in a reverse way, by endlessly diminishing matter. Within the hand that holds this book (or screen) there swirls a storm of uncountable molecules, and within each molecule a storm of atoms, and within each atom a storm of electrons and positrons, photons and neutrons, down and down to quarks that have names like *up* and *strange*, *top* and *charm*, and that in fact are not points of matter at all, but little (ha!) loops of "string" that somehow imply the existence of an endless series of universes that are inevitable, given our math, and inaccessible, given our minds, both necessary and never. And for all of these particles it is quite possible to be here and now ("See . . . I hold it toward you," says John Keats of his "living hand") and there and then (Keats is dead) at the same "time." "It may be," says the physicist Marcelo Gleiser of these subatomic entities of which you, I, and every other observable thing in the universe is made, "that 'exist' is too strong a word."

One can't help but feel awe in the face of all this. But then what? Awe without an end ends in dread, for however much the mind is lit by the fires of that eternal elsewhere, we inevitably fall back into this singular being that, though it matters so much to us, matters not at all in the furnace of infinity. Hence the deepest "spiritual" feeling of our time: dread. If ninety-nine percent of all creatures that have existed are now extinct; if even the most apparently placid natural prospect is in reality a fevered scene of mechanical contest and immeasurable death (it was this that most disturbed some of the first readers of *On the Origin of Species*, that beauty itself became an abomination); if the depth and dimensions of reality are not simply inaccessible to an individual consciousness but inimical to it, then truth and death are but sneering synonyms, and our awe no more meaningful than a sneeze.

But might our awe have a different "end"? Can oblivion really be a means of deeper seeing? If the verb *to exist* is too strong a word for one element of existence, isn't it possible that it's too weak a word for another?

> It should be a rather exhilarating thought that the moment of creation is now—that if, by some unthinkable accident, God's attention slipped, we wouldn't be here. It means that within every circumstance, every object, every person, God's action is going on, a sort of white heat at the centre of everything. It means that each one of us is already in a relationship with God before we've ever thought about it. It means that every object or person we encounter is in a relationship with God before they're in a relationship of any kind with us. And if that doesn't make us approach the world and other people with reverence and amazement, I don't know what will.
>
> —ROWAN WILLIAMS

Another way of saying this is:

maybe death isn't darkness, after all,
but so much light wrapping itself around us—

Or:

> How well the sun's rays probe
> The rotting carcass of a skate, how well
> They show the worms and swarming flies at work,
> How well they shine upon the fatal sprawl
> Of everything on earth. How well they love us all.

Or, and ultimately:

> and fear lit by the breadth of such calmly turns to praise.

Everything in you must bow down. If not to God, then to the goddamned fact of existing at all, "the million-petaled flower of being here," as some gracious angel, through the pen of Philip Larkin, once put it. The stage has enlarged, but the old tensions obtain, and the rescue we need is not from oblivion but from ourselves, "the torment of self-serving demands" that keep creation in an unimaginable past, or keep consciousness in an imprisoning present.

I have long thought—because I have long felt—that the perfections of art implied or even anticipated some ultimate order one need not call God, but could call out to nonetheless; that a feeling that found its true form could align the heart with the stars, make of remote and implacable matter a mirror in which subject and object might see, and even be, each other. "I rhyme to see myself," Heaney wrote in an early poem linking artistic creation with the child's playful calling down a well: "to set the darkness echoing." And perhaps in one sense this understanding of art is not after all so different from C. K. Williams's speculation that our gods grew out of our need to have our achievements—and our amazements—recognized and reflected back to us. Both ideas assume that a work's true end is elsewhere, that there is some *other* needed to fulfill its nature.

What have *I* been wanting all these years when I couldn't stop wanting? Form? Order? Yes, certainly those things, something to both speak and spare the turmoil of my own consciousness, something to protect and preserve me from the ramifying reality of impersonal space and matter long before I had science to confirm those things, and long before I had my own malevolent cells to ram that fact into my heart. But after all this, what I know is that poetry is not enough, and to make it an end rather than a means is not simply a hopeless enterprise but a very dangerous one. "Understand that there is a beast within you / that can drink till it is / sick, but cannot drink till it is satisfied."

Yet it's not that simple. For the paradox—the vital, fatal fact at the heart of human existence—is that with art, as with every truly creative act in life, you must act as if the act itself *were* enough. There can be no beyond. You must spend everything on nothing, so to speak, if nothing is ever to stir for and in you. "If you don't believe in poetry," said Stevens, "you cannot write it." He might have added (and perhaps, implicitly, he did): If you cannot believe in what poetry—in all its forms, even the wordless ones—has revealed to you, you cannot survive it.

And of all those revelations, a certain "sacred weakness," as

Maritain calls it, is key. (*Thank you for my losses* is the prayer that a friend of mine—also a poet, also a patient—found herself bafflingly but joyfully praying recently.) To admit an insufficiency can be to acknowledge the existence of, if not yet to claim full faith in, a healing wholeness, in the way an imperfection can call forth a beauty whose true nature would never have been felt otherwise. Not the imperfections one chooses, like the missing stitch that certain master craftsmen weave into their rugs as an act of piety meant both to imply and appease the original Maker, but the ones forced upon us by necessity or genetics, our physics or our failing cells, which keep us hungering for, and open to, that ultimate order that we cannot in this life inhabit—except in the spots of time that nourish our souls, and haunt our selves, in equal measure. Our only savior is failure.

We spent the night at Eagle Pond Farm. Linda brought fresh-picked blueberries over for pancakes the next morning, but before we ate, she led us out to the old barn to explore. Don was too frail to come with us. I was coughing and hacking from one of the endless respiratory infections I had for years, feeling anxious and awry because of the lack of sleep my lungs had caused. (At one point in my wanderings around the old house, I plucked a book by Ezra Pound from the shelf and found a long, warm inscription to Don from the mad master himself.) I heard the girls clambering around the old stalls and implements, asking if "Donald Hall" (as they unfailingly call him even now) had been in these places, done these very things, as a child. In two weeks Seamus Heaney would be dead, his last words a text to his wife in which he quoted the

Gospel of Matthew: *"Noli timere"* (be not afraid). In four weeks I would be in the hospital with all the bones in my face on fire. In a year, given reprieve by a futuristic drug that came into the world just as I began to go out of it (bless you, my many chemical technicians), I would give a lecture called "Poetry and/as Faith" and a man would stand up afterward to ask why I couldn't just go ahead and drop the "and," since—he tried to put it gently, there was nothing combative at all—it seemed so obvious *that's* where my real faith was. Cries came down from the rafters craving blueberry pancakes *now, now, now*. When we got back inside, "Donald Hall" sat just as we had left him, staring into whatever he was working on as if he hadn't even blinked.

POEM ENDING WITH A SENTENCE FROM JACQUES MARITAIN

It was the flash of black among the yellow billion.
It was the green chink on the chapel's sphere.
It was some rust or recalcitrance in us
by which we were by the grace of pain more here.
It was you, me, fall and fallen light.
It was that kind of imperfection
through which infinity wounds the finite.

—CW

ACKNOWLEDGMENTS

Brief sections of this book have appeared, in different forms, in *The Christian Century*, *Poetry Ireland Review*, and *Poetry*.

The student mentioned on page 92 is Travis Helms.

I am very grateful to my research assistant, Laura Traverse, whose diligence and intelligence have been a great help at every stage of this project.

Deep thanks to Peter Cole, Jonathan Galassi, Ilya Kaminsky, and Danielle Chapman for the close attention they gave to an early draft of this book.

Grateful acknowledgment is also made for permission to reprint the following material:

Reprinted by permission of Farrar, Straus and Giroux: "Third Hour of the Night," from *Star Dust: Poems* by Frank Bidart, copyright © 2005 by Frank Bidart. "Sunlight: Mossbawn," from *Opened Ground: Selected Poems 1966–1996* by Seamus Heaney, copyright © 1998 by Seamus Heaney. "Aubade," from *The Complete Poems of Philip Larkin* by Philip Larkin, edited by Archie Burnett, copyright © 2012 by the Estate of Philip Larkin, introduction copyright © 2012 by Archie Burnett. "Repression," from *Selected Poems* by C. K. Williams, copyright © 1994 by C. K. Williams. "My Stop Is Grand," from *Once in the West* by Christian Wiman, copyright © 2014 by Christian Wiman.

A. E. Stallings, "Momentary." First appeared in *Poetry* (February 2012). Reprinted by permission of A. E. Stallings.

Donald Hall, "Summer Kitchen," from *The Painted Bed: Poems*, copyright © 2002 by Donald Hall. Reprinted by permission of Houghton Mifflin Harcourt Publishing Company. All rights reserved.

Mary Oliver, "White Owl Flies Into and Out of the Field," from *Owls and Other Fantasies* by Mary Oliver, published by Beacon Press Boston. Copyright © 2003 by Mary Oliver. Reprinted by permission of the Charlotte Sheedy Literary Agency Inc.

Danielle Chapman, "In Order," from *Delinquent Palaces*, copyright © 2015 by Danielle Chapman. Published 2015 by TriQuarterly/Northwestern University Press. All rights reserved.

Craig Arnold, "Meditations on a Grapefruit," from *Poetry* (October 2009), copyright © 2009 by Craig Arnold. Reprinted with the permission of the Permissions Company, Inc., on behalf of the Estate of Craig Arnold.

Susan Howe, "The Disappearance Approach" (seven-line excerpt), from *That This* by Susan Howe, copyright © 2010 by Susan Howe. Reprinted by permission of New Directions Publishing Corp.

Denise Levertov, "A Cure of Souls," from *Poems 1960–1967* by Denise Levertov, copyright © 1964 by Denise Levertov. Reprinted by permission of New Directions Publishing Corp.

Denise Levertov, "Our Bodies" (fourteen-line excerpt), from *Poems 1960– 1967* by Denise Levertov, copyright © 1966 by Denise Levertov. Reprinted by permission of New Directions Publishing Corp.

Juan Ramón Jiménez, epigraph from *The Complete Perfectionist: A Poetics of Work*, copyright © 2011 by Swan Isle Press. Spanish original copyright © 2011 by Los herederos de Juan Ramón Jiménez. Translation copyright © 2011 by Christopher Maurer. All rights reserved.

A. R. Ammons, "The City Limits," copyright © 1971 by A. R. Ammons. "He Held Radical Light," copyright © 1969 by A. R. Ammons. "Hymn," from *The Selected Poems, Expanded Edition*, copyright © 1987, 1977, 1975, 1974, 1972, 1971, 1970, 1966, 1965, 1964, 1955 by A. R. Ammons. Used by permission of W. W. Norton & Company, Inc.

Jack Gilbert, "They Will Put My Body into the Ground," from *Monolithos: Poems 1962 and 1982* by Jack Gilbert, copyright © 1963, 1965, 1966, 1977, 1979, 1980, 1981, 1982 by Jack Gilbert. Used by permission of Alfred A. Knopf, an imprint of Knopf Doubleday Publishing Group, a division of Penguin Random House LLC. All rights reserved.

Wallace Stevens, "The Planet on the Table," from *The Collected Poems of Wallace Stevens* by Wallace Stevens, copyright © 1954 by Wallace Stevens and copyright renewed 1982 by Holly Stevens. Used by permission of Alfred A. Knopf, an imprint of the Knopf Doubleday Publishing Group, a division of Penguin Random House LLC. All rights reserved.

Mark Strand, "A.M.," from *The Continuous Life* by Mark Strand, copyright © 1990 by Mark Strand. Used by permission of Alfred A. Knopf, an imprint of the Knopf Doubleday Publishing Group, a division of Penguin Random House LLC. All rights reserved.